A WORLD OF FINE DIFFE
The Social Architecture of a Moder

A WORLD OF FINE DIFFERENCE

The Social Architecture of a Modern Irish Village

Adrian Peace

University College Dublin Press
Preas Choláiste Ollscoile Bhaile Átha Cliath

First published 2001 by University College Dublin Press,
Newman House, 86 St Stephen's Green, Dublin 2, Ireland
www.ucdpress.ie

© Adrian Peace 2001

ISBN 1 900621 59 2 (hardback)
1 900621 60 6 (paperback)

All rights reserved. No part of this publication may be reproduced,
stored in a retrieval system, or transmitted in any form or by any
means, electronic, photocopying, recording or otherwise
without the prior written permission of the publisher

British Library Cataloguing in Publication Data
A catalogue record for this title is available from the British Library

Typeset in Ireland in 10/12 Sabon and Palatino by Elaine Shiels, Bantry, Co. Cork
Printed in Ireland by ColourBooks, Dublin

For Anna, Mika and Sam

CONTENTS

Acknowledgements	ix
1 Introduction: 'A Different Place Altogether'	1
2 Country, Village and Pier	14
3 Regional Relations and Local Identities	31
4 Difference and Dispute	49
5 The Generosity of Community	67
6 Fierce Needle and Fine Craic	86
7 The Politics of Powerlessness	106
8 Conclusion	122
Notes	138
Bibliography	144
Index	151

ACKNOWLEDGEMENTS

The research for this book was supported by the University of Adelaide, the Australian Research Council, and the Adelaide Research Centre for the Humanities and Social Sciences (at the University of Adelaide) which granted me a teaching release award for the second semester of 1999. I am obliged to these institutions, and to Ingrid Slotte, Charmaine McEachern and Susan Magarey, who helped me take full advantage of a semester free from undergraduate teaching.

Since I have been researching and writing on Ireland for several years, I have built up many debts to friends and colleagues who have commented on seminar papers, draft essays and working chapters. To some I am especially grateful for many conversations on anthropological topics with which they were usually more familiar than I was, and they are Nigel Rapport, Lee Sackett, Gísli Pálsson, Roy Fitzhenry, Kay Milton, and Michael Allen. I am especially obliged to Hilary Tovey, Chris Curtin and Nuala O'Faolain who read the penultimate version of the manuscript, and made many informed suggestions to which I have tried to do justice. Barbara Mennell, the executive editor of University College Dublin Press, has been thoroughly encouraging and considerate ever since I appeared, entirely unannounced, at St Stephen's Green with a manuscript in my bag.

My greatest debt is to the people of whom I write in the following pages. At all times, they have been generously accommodating to the Australian family which kept appearing so unexpectedly in the midst of their community. I have taken at face value their constant exhortation to 'tell it like it is'. Finally, I am grateful to my family. My wife Jane has been with me whenever I have done research in Ireland, and she has been my harshest critic all the while. Our children came to know this community when they were all quite young. Over the years they have become far more familiar with it than I, so it seems more than appropriate that this book is theirs.

Adrian Peace
Co. Clare
September 2000

1

INTRODUCTION: 'A DIFFERENT PLACE ALTOGETHER'

This is a political anthropology of the processes whereby a small Irish community[1] maintains its sense of social distinction, notwithstanding the comprehensive process of modernisation to which it has been subject in the late twentieth century. Inveresk has been economically and socially transformed over the past 25 to 30 years – as is generally the case in rural Ireland[2] – to the extent that significant change is inscribed on every corner of the community. It is unambiguously stamped on many of its buildings; it indelibly marks the careers of its adult residents; it pervades all relations of consequence, whether economic, political, or religious; and it regularly surfaces as a topic of conversation. Yet despite the extent of this sustained induction into modernity, Inveresk retains a strong, indeed pervasive, sense of its own distinct identity, of being a special place in the world. Notwithstanding the many external forces which threaten to breach and subvert it, this sense of distinction is articulated with pride and the residents work hard to sustain it.

The aim in the following pages is to detail how Inveresk people prosecute this politics of identity under normal and not-so-normal circumstances. The residents say that 'this is a different place altogether' from others in the vicinity and considerably further afield, for although at times they can be unswervingly parochial, most are well acquainted with other villages and towns in the county. At least in the first instance, this distinctiveness arises from the diversity of the community's economic base. Although the adult population is only about 450 for most of the year, Inveresk's economy is considerably more complex than one might reasonably anticipate from its population size; it is assuredly more diverse than that of neighbouring communities. What is important is that the major components of farming, fishing, and small business are concentrated in distinct niches of the local landscape, because out of this association between discrete, designated places, and specific, different means of livelihood, quite

2 A WORLD OF FINE DIFFERENCE

contrasting codes of interpersonal conduct and, indeed, of personal morality emerge.

DOMAINS OF DIFFERENCE

It is by no means overstating the case to say that marked cultural differences demarcate the three domains – as I shall refer to the particular physical and social spaces on the landscape – from one another. It is crucial to appreciate from the outset, however, how attached Inveresk residents are to the domains in which they reside, work, and (in many instances) take their leisure as well. One of the reasons for this is that the majority have been born and bred in the domain where they now reside, so they are exceptionally familiar with all economic, social, and moral dimensions of it. Even when Inveresk people have left the community for several years, they often return to close by their place of birth and they seem as attached to it as those living nearby who have never been away. When residents move around the community, they will talk about their route and their destination in domain specific terms. When they talk about an individual's personality or a family's conduct, there will frequently be explanatory reference to their place of domicile. When they scrutinise the course of a recent event, the domain in which it occurred will always be of pressing relevance, and when a group or an association with a public purpose newly surfaces, the immediate and invariable question will concern its particular place of origin.

The social dynamics of this localised situation readily bring to mind the argument which Bourdieu advances in *Distinction: A Social Critique of the Judgement of Taste*: 'Social identity lies in difference, and difference is asserted against what is closest, which represents the greatest threat' (1984: 479). It is the juxtaposition of the three domains to which I shall return time and again, because this inescapable proximity means that when the residents of one domain define themselves, they do so through persistent comparison with those in the other two domains. The collective identity of those in one domain is always construed in terms of contrast with, and sometimes in terms of opposition to, the others. As Boon emphasises, social identities are intrinsically comparative, and to elaborate an identity is always 'to play the *vis-à-vis*' (1982: 230–1).[3] Doing this in Inveresk entails observing and reflecting all the time on how one's specific place of residence and work is different and distinct from social life in the two neighbouring domains.

Yet despite these considerations and much else besides, Inveresk people do not refer to the locality as a whole as if it comprises three communities. Rather, what they say of this more extensive space is that 'there's three

INTRODUCTION 3

communities in one 'round here' which is not the same thing at all, since
that quite precise and choice phrasing acknowledges the paramountcy of
Inveresk as a social and political unity which incorporates and encapsulates
its three constituent parts. The enlisting and enveloping space of Inveresk
is talked about as superordinate to its three domains, and it is, I shall
argue, in the way that it is made to encompass them by the constant and
innovative efforts of the residents that its distinctiveness is constituted
from other, more elementary communities in the locality.

Where the boundary between Inveresk and its neighbouring communities is to be drawn is a matter for debate; but it is not all that clear
for that matter where one domain terminates and another begins inside
the community.[4] It is in the nature of this community that such issues are
vague. What is beyond doubt is that incidents, events and happenings
regularly surface to give public, symbolic expression to the coherence
and integrity of Inveresk as a community. It is on such occasions that
Inveresk presents itself both to neighbouring settlements and to the world
beyond as 'a different place altogether'. It is at such times too that the
sense of pride in the community is tangible, for these events can be
interpreted and savoured as proof positive, so to speak, that those
economic and political forces which work to undermine difference and
impose sameness on this community, and other small places like it, have
thus far been kept at bay.

PRACTICES OF EMPLACEMENT

To an anthropologist then, what is ultimately most intriguing about the
everyday politics of Inveresk is the continuous tension between those
relations which express the heterogeneity of the community's parts and
those which celebrate the ethos of the whole. I never heard it suggested
that the community's social diversity was on the decline: quite to the
contrary, I was continually told that it was becoming more complex socially
because of the number of blow-ins moving into the place. But it is everywhere acknowledged that fabricating some kind of social and political
unity out of such internal differentiation is acutely problematic, and this
has long been the case. So when the collective identity of Inveresk is
presented (more or less) distinct and enduring to the world at large, this is
always against a background of local members having themselves sur-
mounted social differences and political divisions of considerable moment.

My concern is to describe the genesis, the form, and the management
of these tensions, and to explain how, in a politically accomplished
manner, the construction of unity within Inveresk is realised. Dealing
with discrete difference whilst constituting a unified face are two sides of

A WORLD OF FINE DIFFERENCE

an intricate politics out of which Inveresk's integrity is reproduced, and I shall argue that particular skills and talents are required in order to do this. It requires a by no means inconsiderable command of the stock of knowledge about the permanent and the irregular relations which make up the social architecture of this modern community. It demands, in other words, considerable awareness of, and sensitivity towards, the significance of place – both in the sense of domain and in the sense of community – in other residents' lives.

I need to make it clear that my concern with such practices of local emplacement precedes the current spate of interest in the anthropology of place and the anthropology of landscape. But this was only because, from the mid-1980s, I found Inveresk people so inordinately attentive to the demarcation of differences between the three domains, and even finer differences within each of them. One would have to be singularly indifferent to the folk emphases within this particular Irish community to imagine that the significance of emplacement could be other than a major part of any anthropological analysis.[5] Nevertheless, I readily endorse the emphases elaborated by Feld and Basso in *Senses of Place* (1996), for as they rightly point out, it is not difficult to pass over the significance of place per se in social life just because it can appear so mundane and taken for granted. Precisely because this has been so often disregarded, not least in the anthropology of Ireland in which relations of place and identity have scarcely been touched upon, it is valuable to be reminded that the lives which people live and the contexts in which they live them are inseparable.[6]

The important theme in the anthropology of place is that over time spatial sites take on social meanings and acquire symbolic properties which are centrally important to the individual and collective identities which people ground, elaborate and refine in those sites.[7] Any generalising account of social landscapes is likely to gloss or miss altogether the significance of these meanings and the influence of these symbols because they are so context specific and situationally precise. The analytic imperative becomes to work out 'the cultural processes and practices through which places are rendered meaningful – through which, one might say, places are actively sensed' (Feld and Basso, 1996: 7). In this small and diverse context of Inveresk, the concern is 'to describe and interpret some of the ways in which people encounter places, perceive them and invest them with significance' (Feld and Basso, 1996: 8).

I also need to make it clear that, whilst this is for the most part a study of local-level developments in which parochial issues loom large, these are inseparable from regional processes of political economy and how Inveresk's residents interpret and respond to them. For whilst it may be true that the

INTRODUCTION 5

majority of residents, especially the older generation, have not moved far from Inveresk even for brief periods in their lifetimes, the extent to which the community has been recently subject to the influence of broader economic and political forces ensures that all have a keenly developed sense of exogenous factors affecting their lives. They can also anticipate to a degree the prospects which these hold out for them. These are not easily summarised, but there is only one recurrent thread to which I want to draw attention at this stage, and it is quite straightforwardly the threat of sameness, that is the prospect of an increasing social homogeneity inside the community and its becoming more like its neighbours as a result of centralised and uncontestable forces at work outside it.

THE THREAT OF SAMENESS

Especially towards the end of my final period of fieldwork (1993), it seemed appropriate to broach specifically the issue of future prospects. How did people feel about their future as individuals or as members of the community within the medium to longer term? What was striking was a marked degree of pessimism, even amongst those who had distinctly prospered from economic and social modernisation. This pessimism was considered warranted on the grounds that, for example, local producers were already being pressured to provision much the same commodities, many new dwellings under construction looked essentially the same, regional department stores and supermarkets made much the same goods available to all, the educational system enforced an unwelcome degree of uniformity on pupils at all levels, and finally the mass media seemed to wield an inordinate capacity to impose a narrowness of thinking which could not do otherwise than threaten the diversity of opinion which places like Inveresk consider themselves adept at fostering.[8]

Clearly this is to paint a picture with very broad strokes, but this concern with the prospect of economic and social differences being inexorably eroded is revealing. Even though these informal exchanges were mainly about the future, in these world views there were already indications that the rapidly compounding centralisation of economic, political and cultural power should be recognised as a matter for popular concern. In anthropological circles, this kind of interpretation of global processes has been fairly thoroughly dismissed. Often enough on the basis of slender ethnographic evidence, it is now widely contended that recent technological, economic and political developments have encouraged rather than eroded, for example, the expression of cultural diversity, the generation of cultural hybridity, the expansion of cultural creolisation, and so on.[9]

6 A WORLD OF FINE DIFFERENCE

I suspect that most people in Inveresk would find these emphases rather unconvincing as, I confess, I myself often do.[10] Be that as it may, the relevant point is that in such circumstances the attractions of belonging to a community like Inveresk are indeed pronounced, for here the articulation of social heterogeneity and the savouring of social differences continue. But now it has to be done in a somewhat conscious, deliberate, and even at times calculating way, precisely because exceptional pressures from outside are already being felt. They may not be well down the track in this peripheral context, but the signs for the future are considered to be there. In this light, the spirit of this distinctive and unique community cannot be taken for granted as earlier generations (including the immediately preceding one) have done. It is considered increasingly necessary to be, if not exactly vigilant,[11] certainly deliberate and conscientious about keeping alive the sense of belonging to this particular place at this particular time.

The preliminary point to emphasise, therefore, is that this kind of community concern has to be drawn together and mobilised into collective action in ways which are culturally appropriate to this specific situation. There are basic transactional matters of political organisation and representation which have to be addressed, but which more pheno-menological approaches to the anthropology of place are inclined to pass over. These are especially problematic in a small place like Inveresk, which is pervaded by a fierce spirit of egalitarianism and an almost remorseless opposition to political hierarchy. This means that just about any attempt at leadership in Inveresk is difficult. It is frequently hazardous in reputational terms, it can become enormously time-consuming, and it is possible to get drawn into issues which those involved would far prefer to avoid altogether, so that even the organisation of events which aim to articulate clearly a sense of belonging to the community can flounder without much difficulty. In other words, the problem of coming to terms with Inveresk's egalitarian ethos has to be added to the problem of surmounting the cultural differences between domains. Both concerns are inescapable because they are built into the fabric of everyday life.

PARAMETERS OF INTERPRETATION

There are three basic points to be made about the following analysis, the first of which is that the parameters of this description and interpretation are narrow. The concern is with the politics of Inveresk alone: there is no warrant here to extend its findings to a broader cross section of Irish society. The point warrants emphasis because ambitious generalisation from the particular case study has been such a marked feature of the anthropology of Ireland in the past.[12] The single community has been made to serve as a window onto a much broader collectivity such as 'the west of Ireland', 'the ethnic Irish', or even 'Irish society' in its entirety. This generalising tendency was especially pronounced in the 1970s and early 1980s when communities considered characterised by social disorganisation and collective anomie provided the apparent justification for describing more extensive entities as, for example, 'culturally pathological' or 'in a virtual state of psycho-cultural decline' (Scheper-Hughes, 1982: 5).

It was not surprising that social analysts in Ireland took exception to the depiction of their society in the apocalyptic terminology of break-down, decay and anomie, and some reacted with a serious and justifiable questioning of the anthropological presence in Ireland.[13] I have argued elsewhere that, with the benefit of hindsight, such analyses revealed much more about the positioning of the discipline of anthropology in the power relations between centre and periphery than they informed us about the communities under study.[14] In relation to the present account, however, the relevant issue is that I do not see Irish society, or any particular part of it, including the west of Ireland, to be a 'small and homogeneous . . . culture area' (Scheper-Hughes, 1982:14). To assume a marked degree of cultural homogeneity in this fashion is to erase precisely those social variations which are of significance to the people themselves, and which should be of consequence to the social analyst as well. It is much more challenging (and probably satisfying too) to approach Ireland as a richly diverse and heterogeneous economic and political landscape, a multi-plicity of spaces and places in which the proliferation of cultural difference is the order of the day.

Nor do I consider individuals in this complex landscape to be carried along by a hegemony of culture. This is my second point of departure: individuals and families in Inveresk are to be approached as self-conscious, self-critical and reflective agents who are constantly constituting their own cultural experience in ways which give full, meaningful expression to the identities of difference which constitute the building blocks of commu-nity. Here it warrants especial emphasis that Inveresk's is a predominantly petit bourgeois population, which is in substantial part what makes its politics so intriguing. The anthropology of British communities has, of late, inclined to shy away from questions of class.[15] This is not feasible in Ireland, even though the petite bourgeoisie in Western Europe as an enduringly significant rural class has always created analytic problems for Marxist and non-Marxist sociologies alike. It is a class which is difficult to define categorically (Wright, 1989): it is a class which has proved difficult to theorise (Poulantzas, 1973a, 1973b); and it has proved peren-nially problematic in terms of empirical investigation (Bechhofer and

8 A WORLD OF FINE DIFFERENCE

Elliott, 1976, 1981). These are problems as germane to the present study as any other: it is the petite bourgeoisie, not the peasantry, which arguably warrants the appellation 'the awkward class'.

For the moment, the straightforward consideration is that Inveresk's population is predominantly composed of self-employed men and women who own the productive property from which they and their dependants mostly realise their livelihoods. As Bechhofer and Elliott maintain in relation to petit bourgeois populations generally: 'The one thing they all have – the crucial thing – is petty productive property, and it is a property with which they work themselves' (1981: 183). Whether the specific occupation is that of farmer, fisherman, publican or shop owner, the rank of self-employed property owner is a commonplace one in Inveresk, and from that much else flows in terms of their attachment to place and their concern with identity and status.

The third basic point is that although I have resided in Inveresk for almost three years (1983, 1988 and 1993), what follows remains no more than one anthropologist's account of a particular community. It concentrates on very select processes which are illustrated and are informed by equally specific incidents and events. These are not the concerns which I first set out to study. My initial ambition was to begin an economic anthropology of a modernising agricultural area,[16] albeit one which (for various reasons) was not to be restricted to farming, hence my eventually settling in Inveresk. So for quite some time in my first year of research, I acquired a substantial amount of (admittedly, relatively dour) empirical material which is not specifically detailed but is nevertheless put to frequent use in the following pages.

As that project unfolded, I became increasingly aware of, and bound up in, the relations between place, identity, individual and community which are explored here. But I hesitate to describe my mode of data collection in the usual confident terms of anthropological inquiry (for example, as participant observation). Geertz has written perceptively of what is required to unpack and explore the meanings of place in people's lives. But what he has to say equally applies to the ethnographer who also focuses on the significance of individual and community identities – which are, of course, conspicuously place-related matters. 'Ethnographical tact', Geertz asserts, is demanded under such circumstances because:

> No one really has a theory of (place). No one imagines it is some sort of data to be sampled, ordered, tabulated and manipulated. To study place, or more accurately, some people or other's sense of place, it is necessary to hang around with them – to attend to them as experiencing subjects, as the responsive sorts of beings for whom, in Casey's words, 'the world becomes bedecked in places' (1996: 260).[17]

INTRODUCTION 9

'Hanging around' describes with a fair measure of accuracy how the research reported on in this book was conducted. I hung around on boats, on farms, on street corners, and in other people's kitchens. Most of all, I hung around in bars mainly because so many other male residents did that too. Presenting these people as 'experiencing subjects' is assuredly my main intention, since I presume Geertz to mean by this a focus on the way in which people imaginatively acquire and articulate a sense of the places in which they live, and how they build out of those experiences ideas about the individual self, the identity of the family, and the nature of community as a broader collectivity.

Whether I display the necessary tact, 'ethnographic' or otherwise, I am considerably less certain. For whilst I have held back on publication (by giving precedence to other writings), changed many personal details (but without, I hope, altering the substance), and (with great reluctance) suppressed several key events which transpired during and between my periods of residence – much of this with a view to concealing the true identity of Inveresk and individuals within it – at the end of the day I incline to Rabinow's view that all anthropology entails some measure of symbolic violence, and I fail to see how it could be otherwise. It is, as Rabinow candidly acknowledges, 'inherent in the structure of the situation' (1977: 130). Hastrup elaborates this realistic position as follows: 'We hardly respect our informant's right to fall silent. Probing into cultural silences may be merely a symbolic act of violence, but it is violence nonetheless. For all our rhetoric about dialogue, ethnographic practice requires intrusion and, possibly, pain' (1992: 123).

It will already be evident that this attempt to explore the specifics of place, identity, and community in an Irish setting extends upon the anthropological concern with locality and localism which has emerged over the past ten to fifteen years as a major focus in European anthropology.[18] Nadel-Klein provides a succinct definition of localism:

> [It] refers to the representation of group identity as defined primarily by a sense of commitment to a particular place and to a set of cultural practices that are self-consciously articulated and to some degree separated and directed away from the surrounding world (1992: 502).

She then summarises the prevalent situation in British ethnography as follows:

> Localism has long been a strong contender with class as a dominant theme in depictions of Great Britain, both popular and scholarly . . . One might even say that if the dominant theme of Mediterraneanist discourse has been 'honour and shame,' as Herzfeld points out (1987: 11), then its British equivalent has been localism (1992: 502).

10 A WORLD OF FINE DIFFERENCE

Recent work by Rapport (1993) in particular has taken further this fine-grained focus on local social practices and local world-views, even though this analytical direction has by no means gone unchallenged.[19] It warrants acknowledgement that as a result this genre of European ethnography is somewhat distinguishable from the discipline's distinctly late modern concerns elsewhere with cosmopolitans and creoles, diasporas and dispersals, routes and refugees, and all the other populations and processes which are considered integral to, and illustrative of, late capitalist and globalised relations at the advent of the new millennium.[20] Rather than see this as a negative feature, however, I would argue that it serves the useful purpose of reminding us as anthropologists – and perhaps others – that, notwithstanding many rhetorical claims to the contrary (Marcus, 1992), even in Europe (and especially, one imagines, in rural Europe) the majority of people do not routinely travel very far, they remain profoundly attached to the locales in which they have been raised, and they remain surrounded by those whom they have known from birth.

Naturally it is the case that residents of Irish villages on the scale described in the following pages travel overseas to work or as tourists. A substantial minority of Inveresk folk have worked elsewhere in Ireland and in England; its inhabitants increasingly take their vacations on the continent, some in the United States; and members of half-a-dozen of the households described in this book have stayed with my family and myself on the other side of the world to Inveresk. These experiences too reinforce the point that this locale is unequivocally integrated in the wider political economy. But the residents fall far short of the perpetually mobile, increasingly rootless, identity-seeking migrants with which some anthropologists fill the category of the global ecumene. They know exactly where home is, they are aware with equal assertiveness to which community they belong, and they share these certainties with many others elsewhere in rural and urban western Europe. This makes it all the more imperative to do ethnography on solid, even conventional lines; it makes all the more relevant Pálsson's insistence a few years ago 'that anthropology returns to its classic concern with the ability to listen to other people's accounts, and the willingness to participate in natural discourse' (1993: 3).[21]

In the next two chapters, which establish the ethnographic groundwork for the remainder, the predominant concern is with the places inside Inveresk's boundary with which most residents primarily identify. Since Inveresk as a community is not most residents' paramount point of reference, it is with the composition of its three domains that the analysis has to begin. Chapter 2 details how each domain is economically and socially organised, and the cultural differences between them. Chapter 3 expands on this by detailing how the core means of livelihood in each domain is

INTRODUCTION 11

differentially articulated with the political economy of the region. This is followed by discussion of the importance of certain well-established families in personifying the qualities considered to distinguish the three domains from one another.

The focus in chapter 4 is on how the collective identities associated with domains are played out in the course of everyday life. This requires concentration on the importance of conflicts within the community, including the tensions arising from residents' petit bourgeois concerns with status and prestige. These predominantly familial conflicts are an integral part of the differences between domains: they confirm how different local codes of interpersonal conduct can be. But these many-sided disputes establish, somewhat paradoxically, that Inveresk as a whole can be considered a moral community, a critical property for providing a basis on which collective political efforts can build.

This process is addressed in chapter 5 where analysis is devoted to the integrative, inter-domain influence of gossip and scandal. Initially I adopt the conventional view that it is through such informal discursive mechanisms that a sense of community is generated. But the main proposition is that gossip and scandal are of consequence in the composition of increasingly refined narratives about individuals, their networks, and the circumstances which surround them. The details of these storylines are drawn upon when residents from throughout Inveresk engage in actions which express their moral obligation to one another. They articulate the sense of moral responsibility which is an integral part of belonging to the community as a whole.

Chapter 6 concentrates on the stratagems adopted by leaders of the community's associations to foster collective interests further. Such associations encounter considerable difficulty in presenting themselves as representative of Inveresk as a whole, and thus worthy of support from across the community. But some are notably successful, and the initial concern is to detail the political skills and tactics required to elicit such wide-ranging support. The main point is that the public events mounted by some of these associations are replete with symbolic importance, and it is their iconic qualities which are drawn out. They are important enough to be explored further in chapter 7, but this is done by way of specific contrast with the enduring difficulties which inhabitants have in attracting the attention of those who rule from a distance to the community's need for state support. This contrast, it is proposed, explains the widespread sense of political alienation in Inveresk; but it also reinforces the petit bourgeois emphasis on self-help which has always been pivotal to the inhabitants' response to social change.

12 A WORLD OF FINE DIFFERENCE

Finally, by way of conclusion I consider what local studies like this one still have to contribute to the anthropology of an increasingly urbanised Ireland. I suggest that they can provide particular insight into the complexities of structured inequality in the Republic, as well as facilitating a critical approach to some of the themes encountered in macro-perspectives on the condition of late modernity.

'A QUEER PLACE ALTOGETHER': THE VIEW FROM OUTSIDE

No claim, then, is being made about Inveresk as somehow typical or representative of a wider cross section of Irish society; and although this is a small community, nor is the account put forward as a comprehensive one either. In the first instance, its justification is on comparative grounds: whilst the importance of space and place, identity and community, have been explored over the past decade or so in a number of localised European settings, the anthropology of Ireland has contributed only marginally to this literature. Irish ethnography scarcely figures, for example, in recent significant compilations of west European ethnography,[22] and the last monograph length community study was Eipper's account of 'the ruling trinity' in Bantry, published in 1986. Having made that acknowledgement, the ambition is more than simply to help rectify this imbalance in the literature. The important issue is one of perspective: I am concerned to approach the inhabitants of this particular place as committed and responsive agents of change under conditions of late modernity, as reflective political actors who are creating the fabric of their economic and cultural world quite as much as it is being made for them by external forces. As much through the expression of social difference as through agreement over common interests, they constitute the meanings and the significance of place which are integral to their individual and collective identities. The analysis stands or falls according to whether or not it explains plausibly these social and political practices.

To give some preliminary sense of Inveresk's distinctiveness as a modern community, let me first recount a conversation with a farmer from a community about three miles distant, whom I chanced on one evening in 1993 at the home of a prominent farming family inside Inveresk. I had been interviewing the head of this farm household when the visitor arrived to conclude some business. Since we left our host at the same time, we walked together in the half-light of dusk towards the centre of the community. The farmer, a bachelor in his late thirties and owner of about 55 acres, was certainly curious about my research, but above all he wanted to know how I found living in Inveresk. I assured

INTRODUCTION 13

him I was comfortable, that my work was going well, and that people were helping me along nicely.

But whatever I said, he wanted to know more, until – catching me off-guard, for I had quite failed to anticipate where this conversation was going – he commented: 'Well, I'm indeed interested to know all that, and I congratulate you on your settling in, for I can't imagine living in this place for a minute'. He gestured around: 'Where I'm from, we think this is just a queer place, a place full of really queer people'. He paused and then went on: 'Hereabouts, they're always at each other's throats, bitching and fighting between themselves, nothing like where I come from where it's quiet-like, where people just get along. And as for the fishing folk hereabouts . . .'. He seemed lost for words at this point, and so resumed his condemnation of Inveresk as a whole: 'The people hereabouts, all they're interested in is themselves. They're just obsessed, just obsessed altogether, with one another'.

What was telling about this exchange was that I had never met this man before, yet he was prepared – I might equally have written that he was primed – to come out with this hostile depiction of Inveresk. But it was actually one (although usually less strongly expressed) which I had encountered time and again during the course of my residence there, and it usually took more or less the same course, notably the emphasis on endemic tension and dispute inside Inveresk by comparison with the 'quiet-like' nature of neighbouring communities, all of which are – and this is especially significant – dominated by farming alone. So from beyond its boundary, the community is undoubtedly considered distinctive: it is condemned as a tough little place, a locale in which people are always 'bitching and fighting' within their ranks. 'Obsession with one another' is considered almost a way of life.

Yet note that Inveresk is nevertheless being talked about as a single community, a place which is more than the sum of its parts, a place which somehow manages to transcend the differences which proliferate within it. Even those who condemn Inveresk from outside will nevertheless concede, either implicitly or explicitly, that it can demonstrate a degree of unity and cohesion which is, by any standards, impressive. In order to realise how much of a political achievement this is, there is no other point at which to begin than the three specific places within which people conduct their everyday lives.

2

COUNTRY, VILLAGE AND PIER

There are two routes into Inveresk. The first is called the Low Road: it is at sea level, and about two miles out from the community it is possible to see much of the settlement suspended above the shoreline on one side of Inveresk Bay. The second route, which people refer to as the Hill Road, passes through several miles of rolling countryside before arriving at the brow of a hill from which there is an open view to the other side of the bay. From the juncture of these two minor roads, a single route passes through the village, after which it follows the coastline before branching away from Inveresk's small harbour to terminate abruptly above the high cliffs.

The road ends at this point because virtually all of Inveresk is situated on a thick thumb of land pushing out to sea, a feature of the regional landscape of which people make a good deal. Long-term residents often remark that living in this peripheral place has always been 'a bit like living on an island'. But this is not just a matter of physical location. It is because, local people proclaim with not a little satisfaction, they can be exceedingly insular in their habits, especially in their behaviour towards blow-ins (who have assumed more or less permanent residence) and strangers (who are only passing through).

It takes no more than half an hour to walk from the countryside to the cliffs, but within that time one traverses the three distinctly different domains from which the community is made up. It is not necessary to be familiar with the local landscape to discern the physical differences between the domains. Even though the physical boundaries between them are not noticeable, there is evident variation in the means of livelihood in which residents are chiefly involved. What is important, however, is the extent of social differentiation which results; this cannot be read off from contrasts in landscape usage.

Considering its small scale, the cultural differences within Inveresk are remarkably pronounced, and they influence just about every social and political aspect of communal experience. In substantial part, these differences are the product of historical forces: they are, at the least, the result of several decades of development and change in the economic activities concentrated in each domain. In equal part, they are of the current residents' own making, the result of the choices that people make on a day-to-day basis as to how they will order their lives. Whatever the relative weight of past and present, however, it is within their respective domains that well-established families and long-resident individuals have developed, and continue to develop, their distinctive identities. Here they share the affective and sentimental bonds which make these places 'truly meaningful' (Feld and Basso, 1996: 7).

THE COUNTRY: FROM RESERVE TO RESTRAINT

The countryside surrounding the small settlement and extending back across its hinterland is low-lying downland, devoid of substantial stands of trees yet much divided by stone walls, thick hedgerows, and boreens which are the rough tracks leading to the locality's farms. Most farmhouses and their farmyards stand well apart from neighbouring properties, but where the lie of the land allows some shelter from powerful winds which come in off the sea, two or three properties are occasionally concentrated together.

Dairy farming and tillage are the two uses to which this fertile land is put. Most dairy cows are Friesians but other breeds are sometimes included in the herd to raise the butter fat content of the farm's total milk yield. Where land is devoted to tillage, the choice of root and cereal crops turns on prevalent prices and the farmer's judgement of their likely direction in the future. Barley production is significant in this area as is sugar beet because both are sound sources of income, even though growers have to pay substantial sums to agricultural contractors who carry out most of the mechanical work.

This is the domain which all Inveresk folk refer to as the country and there is variation between the farm households located in it. Out of the total 25 farms spread across the hinterland, 14 are run by farmers who reside on the property with their wives and children (in several instances also caring for an aged relative); five are in the hands of pairs of brothers, and one in the hands of a brother and sister (these are mostly members of the older generation who have never married); and five are owned by bachelors living alone (only one of whom is under the age of 40). The majority of properties have been passed down to the present generation through the male line. There are only three exceptions to this, all of which arose from the failure of the previous generation to produce a male heir;

but in each instance a daughter married a spouse of farming stock from outside the locality, and these men assumed control of the farms.

Just as there are significant differences in the composition of farm households, there are variations in the size of the properties. Two farms are less than 25 acres in size, whilst 12 fall within the range 25 to 49. Four farms incorporate between 50 and 74 acres, there are none between 75 and 99, and a further four are between 100 and 124. The three largest farms are between 125 and 150 acres in size. Not all these larger acreages are located within the townland of Inveresk.[1] After raising to its limit the productivity of the inherited home farm, several owners have purchased substantial takes (that is, parcels of land) at increasing distances from the community. They have had to do this because, since the thick thumb of the townland is bounded on two sides by the sea, the expansionist farmer can only purchase land in a westerly direction and not to all points of the compass.

Overriding all these considerations is the crucial point that each of these privately owned farms is reliant on the collective labour of those who reside there to render it a commercial enterprise. The resident family is also the unit of productive labour, an equilibrium which has been arrived at by several developments, the first being investment in agricultural technology. In the 1950s, all farms except the smallest had one, two or more labourers under their roof. With the full-scale rationalisation of agriculture, the new technology displaced all wage labour; only horses disappeared more quickly. Second, where the productive capacity of land outstripped available family labour, either small takes were sold off or they were rented out to other farmers under the conacre system.[2]

Third, the use to which current acreage is put is closely matched with the productive capacity of the family unit. The specific concentration on either dairying or tillage, or some combination of both, is determined by the labour power available in the farm household, as well as by its material needs. If a farmer aims to extract the maximum possible financial return, he will devote the farm to dairying. But he then commits himself to continuous labouring and extremely long hours, especially if his land holding is in several takes, and he will need the full support of his wife and older sons. By contrast, although putting land under tillage involves a lot of arduous labour, the total amount of continuous effort is considerably less than with dairy farming. But then the farmer settles for a substantially lower financial return.

In broad terms, the outcome is that those farms owned by bachelors living alone or by pairs of unmarried siblings turn over their land to tillage. Since they are generally getting on in years and have no immediate heirs, they are not driven to maximise their economic return. By contrast, the majority of farms are devoted to dairy farming, or a preponderance of dairying supplemented by tillage, for these units of production are in the hands of young and middle-aged men who commit all their labour to profit maximisation. Their wives not only perform all domestic duties (which unmarried farmers have to provision for themselves), but also often shoulder responsibility for designated activities on the farm, such as the rearing of calves and poultry.[3] The substantial workload which this choice entails for the farmer and his wife is premised on the assumption that a son will eventually take some of the burden off his father's shoulders and ultimately inherit the whole enterprise.

The cultural ethos that flows from these arrangements privileges the family as the natural unit which can work the land to its maximum capacity. Precisely because the land is its sole possession, the farm family is considered most suited to husbanding it effectively: indeed, in these terms property is not so much an object as a relation. It follows that improvements to the property and the development of the family are inseparable processes, and this is crystallised in the inescapable emphasis in farm circles on individual endeavour and shared hard work.

The concern to maximise on financial return is, of course, uppermost in most farmers' scheme of things: farm families live better than most in Inveresk, and they engage in discretionary expenditure (private secondary schooling for some children, for example[4]) which most others would never contemplate. But the stress on hard work is more complex than this. Owning private property means that one shoulders an indivisible responsibility for it. Since Inveresk's farmers are, in effect, only responsible to themselves, they are driven to work harder than most. Unremitting labour is the way to discharge not just the financial but also the moral obligations which go with farm ownership.

Inasmuch as the farm family is economically autonomous from its neighbours, the prospect of its being socially separated is opened up as well. Throughout the country, there is a distinct emphasis on keeping affairs within the family circle, of not allowing loyalty towards this social unit to be compromised in any way. Moderation and restraint are expected from family and individual alike, ostentatious or flamboyant conduct is frowned on, and to act 'quiet-like' is considered to be (as one housewife put it to me) 'the country way of doing things'. Consistent with this is the expectation that the individual will be cautious about being drawn into a wider field of social and political relations. One does not socialise for its own sake but because it might serve some tangible purpose, and when that purpose has been realised, it is appropriate to withdraw once again to the guarded privacy of the farm.

By far the most significant relations maintained by country folk are with the extended family, and this frequently means they are directed away from Inveresk rather than focused inside it. Farmers' wives are usually from farming families elsewhere in the county: their brothers are often farmers in their own right, or at least they remain connected with agriculture; and their sisters have often married into farm families as well. So the close kin of these families are dispersed in predominantly rural locations at some distance from Inveresk. When leisure time becomes available, it is regularly spent with an assembly of relatives amongst whom much of the conversation, at least on the male side, is about agricultural issues.

Celebrations both reflect and reinforce this pattern, so that when, for example, the daughter of one prominent family married in the local church, virtually all the 30 or so guests on her side were relations living at some distance from Inveresk, the majority were of farming stock, and only one neighbour, an elderly widow, was invited to attend. All this was closely observed by other families in the country. One or two neighbours thought the arrangement disappointing, but it was by no means an untoward development bearing in mind the tight-knit familial relations which were routinely maintained.

Farmers and their wives are conscious that this constant concern with the family and its privacy distinguishes them within Inveresk. A much-repeated justification is that it minimises the possibility of serious conflict with other country people. I was frequently warned by farmers as to how easy it is 'to turn a good neighbour into a bad enemy' by sharing confidences about one's family affairs, for nothing is considered so predictable as the likelihood the information would be passed on somehow, and one would mistrust the neighbour henceforth. Be that as it may, there is no doubt that farmers often incline to keep their neighbours at a modest arm's length.

This is not to suggest that the farm family is socially isolated, nor is it to imply that farmers are uninformed about what their neighbours are doing. They remain in touch with one another, they are knowledgeable about how neighbours are faring, and they are even sometimes critical of one another's agricultural practices. Older farmers who concentrate on tillage criticise younger dairy farmers for intensive practices which, they say, put too much pressure on the land. The argument levelled against older tillage farmers is that they are under-utilising their properties, denying highly productive land to dairy farmers who could make better capital use of it. Yet even such modest criticisms are always made quietly. Any kind of face-to-face dispute is strenuously avoided, any kind of irritation or annoyance has to be lived with, for to do otherwise would run too much against the grain. Throughout my fieldwork, I recorded only two serious disputes involving farm families, and their details are unimportant against the fact that neither was much known about beyond the family circle. Elsewhere in Inveresk, such containment of information is out of the question.

THE VILLAGE: BUSINESS AND COMPETITION IN A PUBLIC PLACE

Where the two access routes into Inveresk converge, the village settlement begins, and this is by and large where residents socially situate the boundary between the two domains as well. The village is markedly different from the country which it abuts because this is where the community foregathers socially and politically. Besides being a distinct place in its own right, the village is the hub of all Inveresk's social traffic; the two features are interdependent.

The main reason for this is that most of the area's commercial establishments are situated in the village. In total, the community has five general stores and eight bars (two of these are in hotels). Three of the stores and four of the bars are village enterprises, and one of the stores is also the area's sole victualler. The only garage hereabouts is in the village, and directly opposite it there is a family-owned haulage company. Several other commercial activities are much less conspicuous, including two fish trading companies and two hairdressing businesses, all of which are run from private homes.

Like the farms in the country, village enterprises are all family owned, and the most prominent entrepreneurial families are a permanent presence in the village; they establish its ethos. All shops and bars front directly onto the main street and often they incorporate some living accommodation. Even when they choose not to reside on the commercial premises, entrepreneurs live elsewhere in the village, the only exceptions being the victualler (who is shortly to move from nearby Kilglass into the village) and the garage owner (who owns a bungalow in the country but is constantly at work in the village where he drinks every night).

Quite unlike farm families, however, competition between those who own the shops and the bars can be intense. The shops all trade in much the same narrow range of milk, bread, tinned foods, tobacco, toiletries, and newspapers; and in the bars, the availability of beers, spirits and soft drinks is much of a muchness, as are the prices. These businesses are therefore in direct competition for the same limited custom, and where that custom goes emphatically depends on the social reputation of the shop or bar owner and her or his ongoing relations with customers. In

20   A WORLD OF FINE DIFFERENCE

Inveresk, one no more goes into a shop simply to buy a newspaper than one goes into a bar merely to have a drink.

At times, the competition between village enterprises gets out of control. Donal Flaherty the victualler was fined for leaving deposits of excrement on his rival's doorstep: needless to say, these business folk do not acknowledge each other's presence and have not done so for a long time. An added twist to village competition is that several of the major businesses are owned by different branches of the same resident families. Two of the bars on opposite sides of the main street are owned by brothers who have not had much to do with one another for several years. The remaining bars, almost adjacent to one another, are owned by Máire Neeson and her brother Conor, both of whom are getting on in years. Máire's bar is the smallest and the most disreputable of the lot, which is why it is referred to in somewhat derogatory fashion as the Night Club. But the ownership of both establishments generates a good deal of speculation because Máire is an ageing spinster in poor health, Conor's bar has ceased trading for much of the week and is short of custom at the weekend, and overall the family has fallen from a peak of prosperity about 15 years ago.

By contrast, the entrepreneurially influential Scully family is substantial in size, financially secure and socially tight-knit, as evidenced by the fact that, while Rita Ruane (this is her married name) and her sister Karin (who is unmarried) own the largest village store and one at the pier respectively, they remain constant companions. These enterprises by no means exhaust the Scully properties. Rita and Karin's father's brother, a 67-year-old bachelor who is widely renowned as the family's patriarch, owns several properties inside the community and outside it as well.

So business families such as these enjoy a measure of prosperity, especially where they reinvested profits from a wave of affluence which swept through this and similar communities in the late 1960s and 1970s when the Irish economy was expanding. When the lengthy recession began in the 1980s, some local families were hard hit, but on the whole business people continued to do well. Several have educated their sons and daughters to tertiary level, from which point they have proceeded into salaried employment, and have therefore been lost to Inveresk.

It is important to emphasise that those involved in commerce are not a local elite.[5] They are not socially cohesive, some do not share the affluence of others, and they are as subject to the egalitarian ethos which informs community life as anyone else, although in relation to certain standards of cultural conduct some fare badly. They do not recognise the moral value of community which is so important to others, and this is affirmed in accusations that they are especially 'money minded' and

COUNTRY, VILLAGE AND PIER

'status conscious'. They are accused of considering themselves superior to those engaged in the manual occupations of farming and fishing, despite its being from those sources that their own affluence derives.

It is by no means coincidental that these tensions are concentrated in the same place where money changes hands to a far greater degree than elsewhere. Village transactions entail the handing over of the hard won return from arduous manual work and its perceptible conversion into a comfortable lifestyle for the business folk. They have no right at all under the circumstances 'to act lady-like' or 'to lord it over the rest of us', so when it appears that they try to do so, they are cut down mercilessly. This is where the village begins to earn its specific reputation as 'a right bitchy hole', a place where 'money mindedness' prevails rather than the rendering of proper respect to all concerned. The entrepreneurs are an endless target of gossip which is generated not least by those whom they employ. Their enterprises are virtually the only source of wage-earning inside the community, but the pay is poor, the work is insecure, and it allows others to peer behind the public façade of family business life. The result well bears out country people's argument that there is nothing to compare with working one's property with family labour alone.

Another feature which compounds village tensions is that a number of residents are either in wage-employment at some distance from Inveresk or they are long-term unemployed, yet they receive no acknowledgement as permanent residents: 'the village is run by the business folk for themselves'. In fact, it is not at all uncommon throughout the community for wage-earners and those out of work to be entirely ignored as members of particular social categories. But in the village, unlike elsewhere, an explanation can be found in the self-interestedness of those who own its business establishments.

The ambience of the village as a distinct place is equally marked by its being common terrain for all Inveresk residents, although the social traffic which moves through this space varies according to the time of day. On a weekday morning, women from all three domains visit the shops in one another's company and with their small children: the only men in evidence are those at the garage and the haulage company, or retired men making an early visit to a bar. In the afternoon, the village is quiet until older children return by bus from the market town of Westport, along with adults in private vehicles who work outside the area. By nightfall, the main street is occupied by bands of 'the lads' and young women wandering between village and pier, and by men from throughout the community visiting its four bars and circulating between them. There is no social hierarchy amongst these bars.[6] In the course of an evening, the typical drinker will visit two or three, mixing relationships as well

A WORLD OF FINE DIFFERENCE

as drinks, for the composition and atmosphere of each bar is different from the rest.

What is most important about this changing composition of village space is that the dissemination of local knowledge about the entire community proceeds apace. All these different members of the community – from housewives in the shops to old men in the bars – discourse ceaselessly about current events, recent relationships, and upcoming issues. As members of each category depart the village, they leave behind the conversational traces which can be picked up and added to by the next cohort passing through. These traces can be made to cohere to the ligaments of significant storylines which residents compose about one another, and in which is inscribed the essence of belonging to Inveresk.[7]

The other main reason for this variety of traffic, however, is the concentration of communal resources in the village, the National school (for primary level education only), the community hall, and the Catholic church which stands on the hill overlooking a row of village houses, including the priest's residence. We shall see that social differences within the community at large surface in the context of the National school.[8] Here it suffices to observe that even in the innocuous routine of small children being delivered each morning, these differences can be detected. Mothers from the country arrive by car, drop off their offspring, and immediately return to the separateness of the farmhouse. By contrast, those from village and pier arrive on foot in twos and threes, intently discussing family and neighbourhood affairs.

The formal organisation of the National school clearly expresses the power which the Catholic church exercises over education in Ireland. The school is administered by the priest as chairman of its Board of Management, a hierarchical arrangement with which many have qualms. Equally problematic is the status of the community hall, for whilst this too is on church land, the priest's influence over it is sometimes contested. The hall was the end product of a major cooperative effort over a decade ago, and for some time it seems to have been agreed that the building was the community's responsibility rather than being subject to the priest's direction.

The priest who organised the hall's construction is said, at least in retrospect, to have honoured this understanding. But his successors have not, including the present incumbent, and this has provoked a good deal of tension between himself and residents who regard the power of the church beyond its religious orbit to be anachronistic. As is so often the case in Inveresk, this dispute is also influenced by the ethos of egalitarianism, specifically whether it should apply nowadays to the incumbents of roles which in the past allowed a good deal of power over ordinary

COUNTRY, VILLAGE AND PIER

people, which means not only the priest but also the headmaster. The unfolding storyline on this issue is intriguing, but to follow it closely it is necessary to be onside with the incumbent of a less prestigious role than those under scrutiny, the caretaker of the community hall.

The ambience of the village is less distinctive than that of the other two domains, precisely because it is in so many ways common terrain. But it is quite different from that of the country in that even the most private concerns of its business families are difficult to conceal. There is a sense in which symbolic violence is widespread in the village, for malicious gossip directed against several individuals and families is par for the course. 'A bitchy hole' is a damning label, and it is because of this reputation that country folk often quit the village as soon as their business is done. Alternatively, they retire to the one place they feel at ease, the bar known as the farmers' house. Farmers congregate here because its owner has a long association with country families (they provided his meat supplies when he was the victualler, and he remains an ardent dog fancier), and because he and his wife are considered temperamentally to be 'more country than village', as one of their close friends put it.

From the observer's vantage point, the critical function of the village concerns the flow of local knowledge about parochial matters which constantly passes through it. Even for country people this is important, not least because in the farmers' house they can experience vicariously signal happenings at the pier, the one place which truly respectable farm families avoid contact with altogether.

THE PIER: CAMARADERIE AND CONFLICT

The physical distance from village to pier is less than half a mile, but no one underestimates the social distance between them, still less the cultural divide between pier and country. The distinctiveness of the pier is undeniably pronounced, and this is the product of two major factors: its localised economy is dominated by fishing, and its productive relations, domestic relations and leisure activities are concentrated within a narrowly circumscribed space. Such is their combined influence that pier inhabitants proudly and justifiably proclaim their particularity. Tadgh Brown, who has spent virtually all his 38 years at the pier where he belongs to one of its most prominent fishing families, put it this way: 'We're different all right, the pier's a different place entirely to everywhere else 'round here. We're a real community, nothing like those jumped-up fuckers in the village, we really look after one another – all of the time.'

Inveresk's harbour is small, no more than a few hundred yards in diameter, and it is bounded by a dog-leg harbour wall, a low raking

24 A WORLD OF FINE DIFFERENCE

breakwater, and a pebble strand. In this location are moored what are locally termed big boats which are 25 to 40 foot wooden or metal-hulled vessels, punts which are small fibre-glass dinghies powered by outboard motor, and a number of small leisure craft which disappear with the end of the summer. All the boats in the first two categories, numbering 12 and 11 respectively (these are 1993 figures), are owned by Inveresk fishermen. In addition, there is one 45 foot trawler, but this too is dwarfed by French, Dutch, and Spanish trawlers which occasionally take shelter in Inveresk Bay. The reason given by fishermen for the limited size of their vessels is that the harbour is usually silted up, allowing no draught for larger boats. Outside their ranks, it is said that too many pier people lack the ambition to get ahead, notwithstanding their undoubted fishing expertise.

Whatever the explanation, the small size of the vessels has major productive consequences. Weather conditions frequently bring fishing to a halt for several days, sometimes a week or more. When foreign fleets appear offshore and clear the area of fish, again local fishing is halted for some time. More generally, fish stocks are depleted by comparison with a decade or two previously, so that the financial return from such small boat fishing quite frequently fails to meet household needs. The result is that, regularly or occasionally, Inveresk skippers and sharemen sign up for the dole: they do so for several days or sometimes several weeks, especially during the winter; and often enough they claim dole payments whilst fishing, at least until such time that social security officers decide to enforce the regulations strictly.

There are several types of fishing pursued from the port. The major ones involve fishing with nets or long lines for demersal or pelagic fish either in the bay or between three and 15 miles out to sea. This fishing is done throughout the year from big boats when an owner-skipper will have a crew of two or three on board. By contrast, potting for lobster, prawns and other shellfish is restricted from April through to September. Both types of boat are involved, but they operate on a different scale and in different locations with the coastline reserved for one- or two-man punts. The most lucrative fishing by far comes with the salmon season which is officially restricted to the summer months. Whilst punt owners anchor 100 to 200 yards of nets in the bay, big boat skippers fish with two or three miles of drift nets below the cliffs of Cahergal Head northeast across the bay, or below Murragh Point directly west of the harbour.[9]

Inasmuch as fishing is at all turns a highly cooperative endeavour, on a daily basis the harbour is the site of complex, reciprocal relations between all fishermen, whether skipper-owners or sharemen. Punts, nets, fish boxes and other items of equipment are always in circulation between them, along with engine parts, gaffes, petrol containers (which are used as

COUNTRY, VILLAGE AND PIER

buoys), and so on. Apart from cash loans, the most important resource to be passed back and forth is information because on a day-to-day basis a comprehensive ledger is required on the weather, fish prices, fish buyers, the regional bailiffs, and much more. Every fisherman accesses an up-to-date account of how other boats and their crews are faring, especially concerning the type of fishing in which his vessel is currently engaged or the one to which his boat may switch in coming days. The information is essential, however casually or indifferently it might be accessed, and the most important sources are the two bars immediately above the harbour. Fishermen are in and out of these establishments all the time, but especially at night and over the weekend. Over pints of stout and whiskey chasers, current information is accessed, contributed to, talked about, and pored over; and then it is passed on, but always selectively for this specific stock of knowledge is as valuable as any other factor of production.

There is nothing particular to Inveresk about the way in which fishing draws men together in a complex field of work relations.[10] But in this place its intensity is reinforced and compounded by the residential circumstances of fishing families, most of whom live only a couple of hundred yards from the harbour in old cottages, bungalows, or two rows of council housing which directly overlook the harbour and its bars. The older row of council houses was built in the 1940s, the more recent one in the late 1960s, and in some cases resident families have bought their dwellings and improved them. The physical location of all these properties in relation to the pier ensures that its population works, resides and takes its leisure cheek-by-jowl, an arrangement unparalleled elsewhere in Inveresk, and, it needs to be stressed, one quite incomparable with the spatial arrangements of country folk.

Not all pier residents are dependent on fishing for their livelihoods. In addition to those who own bars and run shops, several households are headed by women and men in other forms of self-employment (as builders, house painters), in wage-employment (in a construction firm or a local pottery), or they are on the dole. From their homes, women generate income from hairdressing, clothes making, house cleaning and pyramid selling.[11] But fishing is the major means of livelihood so that how well, or how badly, fishing families are faring impacts on the material circumstances of others. When the weather is poor or the area has been fished out by foreigners, bar takings fall off markedly and more credit has to be extended in the general stores. The annual transition from summer salmon fishing to the winter concentration on cod, hake and pollock, often means that less money circulates in the pier domain.

Socially, the important consideration is that half-a-dozen long-established and large pier families are involved in the fishing industry, and it is

26 A WORLD OF FINE DIFFERENCE

relations between them that dominate pier life on a regular basis. Typically, these families have several residential branches headed by brothers and/or their older sons. In a number of instances, they have married women from other families in the area before setting up separate households. Alternatively, younger pier men and women have remained in their parents' homes after marriage, and then, after one or two children have been born, they have built an extension to the original dwelling.

As a result, a fisherman and his spouse characteristically reside along-side other fishermen and their wives, some of whom are close kin as well as immediate neighbours. Since pier folk have generally been born and bred in Inveresk or a community nearby, and since few have been away from the locality for more than a few months (for example, on building sites on the Isle of Man), other neighbours are likely to be their long-standing acquaintances as well. The upshot is that close intercourse between pier households is de rigueur, and local women frequently stress an open door arrangement whereby, as I was often told, 'we live in each other's houses all of the time'. Pier women move freely between the domestic space of mothers, sisters, female-in-laws, and friends during the course of a day. Since a substantial percentage have small children, child rearing is widely organised as a joint exercise between different branches of the extended family.

The sociability of the pier is above all pronounced when its bars are full and the residents are collectively in evidence. Friday is pay day at the pier. The fish buyers from the village or outside the community deliver their cheques to the owner-skippers currently supplying them with fish. They are immediately cashed with bar owners (who function as the pier's informal bankers), whereupon each skipper discreetly distributes the shares agreed upon with his crew. With cash in hand, fishermen are now able to establish with a fair degree of accuracy how their boat has fared by comparison with others. But this is not all. Over the weekend, fisher-men and other community residents are accompanied by their wives and girl friends, and live music is laid on by one or other of the pier publicans. It is at such times that the quality of the craic[12] indexes the sense of collective well-being currently prevalent at the pier and elsewhere.

There is another side to pier life, however, and it involves intense competition between boats, open feuds between individuals and families, and on occasion not only the symbolic violence of destructive verbal comment but also physical confrontations which attract the attention of the entire community.

Competition between boats is a fact of everyday life for fishermen, mainly because at the end of each day a crew's degree of success is made comparable with that of others. Each boat's catch is put up on the harbour

COUNTRY, VILLAGE AND PIER

wall to await collection by the fish buyers, and then the comparisons begin, for this is an unavoidably public demonstration of relative productivity. It is also a major catalyst of conflict in that once it becomes known where large catches are being made, other boats will flock to that location, and in the subsequent crowding, nets get tangled, pots become snagged, tempers begin to fray, and hostile comments are thrown back and forth.

The sequence is by no means as mechanical as a brief summary might suggest; a boat may well take a different direction, or stick with its existing marks out at sea since the skipper's intuition tells him to do so. But this is essentially why conflict at sea is so recurrent. It is triggered by the fact that some fishermen operate on a short fuse. It escalates because, once a dispute between boats gets under way, skippers are loathe to back down. (If one acquires a reputation for doing so, it is argued, others will increasingly take advantage of one's purported weakness.) The important point is that skipper-owners are always looking for optimal sites out at sea, and since this is the commons, quite unlike the private farmland of the country domain, there is no way of restricting access to others.

This is why relations between skipper-owners are unpredictable. Two skippers might be observed cooperating closely one week, at each other's throats the next. Similarly fluid are those between boat owners and their sharemen, and this as much on a weekly as a seasonal basis. Men who fish from their own punts during the summer will generally take a berth on a big boat for the winter season. But sometimes the owner of a big boat might decide to work for a share on another owner's vessel. Then again, two big boat owners may pool their gear, technology and knowledge, and take one boat out of the water.

There are different combinations. What remains constant throughout is that all agreements between a skipper and his crew are informally established, and it is always understood that owner–sharemen relations can be broken off, so that the combination of crews in the harbour is subject to recurrent change. A shareman may suddenly decide to move to another boat because the present one is fishing badly, the skipper is exercising poor judgement, the gear is insufficient or worn out, and so on. On the other side, a skipper may sack his sharemen because they are not punctual, avoid dirty jobs, complain too much, or turn up half-drunk. The reasons for social rupture are diverse, it proves difficult to establish what the major reason for dispute is, and it is hard to determine why some quarrels fade away within a couple of days when others prove protracted.

It is also possible that at root such disputes are not about fishing at all, or at least only to a minor degree. Instead they arise and are sustained by interpersonal or interfamilial disputes which have developed on shore and have, as it were, been transported out to sea. In the confined space of

28   A WORLD OF FINE DIFFERENCE

council houses and bungalows, relations inside the predominant extended families are by no means consistently cordial: women fall out with their in-laws, men find themselves at odds with their cousins, or even siblings; and teenagers too generate their own tensions. Alternatively, major disputes break out between extended families and their strung out course becomes a major test of family loyalty.[13] As a result, and often for no perceptible reason, the marked sociability which pervades the pier is disrupted by public outbursts of anger; and in the context of a rowdy bar, following an episode out at sea over access to an optimal fishing mark or snagged salmon nets, a fist fight breaks out.

Precisely because of the multiplex character of relations[14] which exist between fishermen, they are inherently unpredictable. A kinship tie does not necessarily keep tension in check, co-residence can either contain or compound a dispute, and a close friendship between their wives is no guarantee that two skippers will bury the hatchet quickly. In the context of the pier, the situational specifics of relations between fishermen are everything, and for this reason fluidity, uncertainty and unpredictability are the order of the day. This is why relations swing between the poles of cooperation and camaraderie on the one hand, and on the other tension and dispute. This is also why the cultural distinctiveness of the pier in relation to Inveresk as a whole is not only pronounced but is also made much of by its residents. These differences are precisely the place-specific cultural attributes which collectively distinguish them from the rest, and they have no hesitation in making much of them.

DOMAINS OF DIFFERENCE, FIELDS OF FAMILIARITY

It should be clear from these details why its residents refer to Inveresk as 'three communities in one', and why as a result it is so often politically problematic to organise a commonality of purpose and sustain a unanimity of direction amongst residents drawn from the pier, village and country. This is an especially intricate rural place considering its limited population size. It exhibits a degree of internal cultural diversity and heterogeneity which is belied by immediate appearances. The differences are by no means obvious to the casual observer, but the more one resides in this setting, so its relative richness in terms of internal cultural variation begins to surface. At the same time, the differences between domains are evidently likely to pose an obstacle to any attempt at mobilisation across the community as a whole.

By contrast with its neighbours, Inveresk is especially distinctive because they are, for the most part, characterised by a preponderance of farming

COUNTRY, VILLAGE AND PIER

families, which means that they are relatively homogeneous in cultural terms. No other community nearby, for example, has a comparable population engaged in fishing as a means of livelihood; one or two have a handful of fishermen, but their numbers are too insignificant to offset the overwhelming cultural influence of those owning private farms. Nor has any other community within the vicinity anything equivalent to the commercial base which is spread between Inveresk's village and pier. The communities which are closest each have a public house and a couple of small stores; but again, these entrepreneurial interests have nothing akin to the influence which Inveresk's businessmen and women exercise over the village, thus marking it out as social terrain quite distinct from country and pier.

In short, by comparison with Inveresk, other settlements in the region assuredly appear modest and ordinary, and of this its residents make a good deal. Some indication of this was to be found in the reception to my own arrival and my announcement that, as an anthropologist, I hoped eventually to write a book about it. No one considered it at all strange that I proposed to do this. The general response was that I had come to exactly the right place, indeed I could not have made a better choice. I had only been resident for a month when a bachelor farmer, then aged just over 60, collared me in the farmers' house to extract more detail about my line of work. His response was:

> Well, sure enough we're an interesting bunch here all right, far more interesting than any other place 'round here. Oh yes, if you're a writer of some sorts, we'll certainly find something for you to write about. But where would you begin to start when we're all so different from one another?

In sum, in the first instance Inveresk's long-established residents are distinctly attached to their specific places of pier, country and village: it is developments ongoing in these domains which are their prime concern. They identify intimately with these specific contexts, they acknowledge to the full the differences which exist between them, and they reflect on them all the time in the course of the projects which they mount, the conflicts that they get drawn into, and the conversations which constitute the essence of everyday life. The critical consideration is always the juxtaposition of village, country and pier, for this inescapable proximity means that how the members of each domain define and conceptualise themselves always draws on their understandings of what those in the other two domains are, or are not. 'Playing the *vis-à-vis*', to use Boon's succinct phrase once again, is exactly what the constitution of local identities is all about in Inveresk: but in this context, there are – if it can be put this way – two pertinent cultural Others constantly to hand as the identity of a pier resident, a villager, or a country person is being constituted and articulated.

A WORLD OF FINE DIFFERENCE

In certain respects, it is not surprising that people identify so closely with their respective domains, for as I have acknowledged, most continue to reside and work near to the places where they have been raised. Their domains are the social fields they know with exceptional familiarity, and in the next chapter we will look at this in more detail. There are, however, certain external forces which have played, and continue to play, a significant part in the constitution of the differences between domains. These warrant examination before turning to the distinctive identities which are part and parcel of that intense familiarity.

3

REGIONAL RELATIONS AND LOCAL IDENTITIES

Inasmuch as Inveresk is a modernised community, its material base is extensively articulated with the wider region, which means in the first instance that it is wholly integrated into the political economy of Ireland, and in the second that of the European Union. There is no sphere of social life within the community which is free from the hegemony of international economic processes, or the power of institutions which work to extend, consolidate and even mitigate the impact of those processes. But there is nothing uniform about this articulation either. The mechanisms of incorporation and integration are variable, and it is this variability which compounds the cultural differences that make up Inveresk as a distinctive community. Before looking at the details of social identities which are constituted within the three domains, it is first appropriate to explain what forms the impact of these processes of articulation specifically take.[1]

FARM CAPITAL AND THE COOPERATIVE

More than any other economic and social unit in Inveresk, the family farm is the beneficiary of wholesale integration into the international marketplace. These relations have an extended history, but the ones of most contemporary relevance originated in the late 1950s and early 1960s when the modernising impetus of the Irish state was channelled into the transformation of agriculture. In light of the continuing backwardness of the economy relative to the United Kingdom and north-west mainland Europe, the modernisation of agriculture became the state's priority: its structural reform was to be the centrepiece of the internationalisation of the economy as a whole.[2] To that end, a comprehensive and costly infrastructure was established in order to generate more rational patterns of land ownership, more productive use of land (as much as was feasible, a move away from tillage to beef production and

32 A WORLD OF FINE DIFFERENCE

dairy farming), as well as the opening up of new markets inside Ireland and overseas. Agricultural produce was no longer to be exported in a raw state: it was to be subject to a wide range of value-adding processes.

From the mid-1960s to the late 1970s, Irish farming enjoyed boom conditions. Markets for all farm produce in Ireland and overseas expanded and commodity prices were buoyant. Demand for agricultural advisory services was constantly increasing, land values rose across the country, extensive advantage was taken of subsidies and loans as enterprising farmers developed their properties and acquired new land from smallholders who lacked the necessary resources for rationalisation. When Ireland joined the Common Market in 1973, small farmers were effectively declared redundant under the Farm Modernisation Scheme, although many took their time to recognise the fact.

This was the period when Inveresk's farmers as members of a rural class became prosperous for the first time.[3] Prior to this, some had been well-off relative to the community as a whole: by the late 1970s, only a handful of smallholders did not share in this rising prosperity. This was the time when extensions were made to farmhouses, thatched roof milking sheds were replaced with aluminium structures, silage clamps were built adjacent to expanding farmyards, and acreages under tillage (or not yet in use at all) were converted into pasture for growing dairy herds. During the 1970s as a result, consumption patterns within the farmhouse were subject to major improvement. In retrospect, this decade is everywhere regarded as the definitive period of rural change and rising affluence.

Subsequently the rate of material advance slowed considerably because by around 1980 the accumulated debt of the Irish state was so substantial as to enforce major cutbacks to the allowances, grants and subsidies available in peripheral areas like Inveresk. As elsewhere, some farmers had overextended themselves financially by this time, and not only did agricultural prices stabilise and even decline in real value, but overproduction also became a major problem with some commodities. (In 1988, for example, milk quotas had to be frozen indefinitely at 1987 levels.) However, in the region surrounding Inveresk, two factors have continued to be critical in sustaining farm prosperity. First, regional banks have continued to regard farming as the soundest area of investment. In the 1970s when capital was unavailable from the state, it could generally be borrowed from these institutions, and this privileged client status has continued through to the present, albeit on a reduced scale.[4]

Second, the cooperative to which all farmers in this region belong is one of the largest and most enterprising in the Republic. From the mid-1970s, the number of cooperatives in Ireland contracted very quickly, and the more successful had to create a range of new products in order to compete effectively in the Common Market. The cooperative which covers Inveresk was at the forefront of these innovations in value-adding, with the result that it is able to offer a high contract price for regular milk supplies, as well as provisioning all the requirements of its members at favourable cost. The same applies to the national corporations which purchase sugar beet and barley from Inveresk's farmers. Although they have little choice but to sell to these monopolistic bodies, as regular suppliers they do well.

These relations with the state, banks and corporations are undoubtedly complex, but that is not the issue. The key point is that they have facilitated and compounded the relative autonomy of the family farm. Each of these external institutions has dealt with the farm owner as a separate, independent producer with particular problems to address and specific ambitions to realise. On no count have they pressed for structural reorganisation at the level of property ownership and production, nor have the farmers collectively mobilised in relation to these institutions since in the main these relations have proved advantageous to them. Each farmer deals with the corresponding institution as he thinks fit and as it suits his individual interests.

Above all, what is important is the farmers' overall success and accumulated prosperity; for it is on this economic bedrock that the farm family's concern with respectability and rank is founded, and it can be confidently consolidated over time. The sense of self-confidence which comes with a well-secured material prosperity is obvious in the assuredness with which they publicly proclaim their standing and prestige as successful rural entrepreneurs. Their prosperity translates into an open and unambiguous emphasis on being respectable and proper, qualities which are only grudgingly conceded to select others within the community at large. In sum, economic and political forces of distinctly non-local provenance have substantially reproduced the relative autonomy of Inveresk's family farm and the cultural emphases which are strongly articulated from within it on a day-to-day basis.

THE LIMITS OF COMMODITY SUPPLY

The economic and social circumstances of village businessmen and women have also been substantially moulded by external forces and institutions. But in the case of those who own public houses and shops, it is the centralisation of regional control in the hands of an increasingly smaller number of commodity suppliers which is important.

Again the point is a comparative one. It has already been mentioned that in the post-war years there were more commercial establishments in

34   A WORLD OF FINE DIFFERENCE

Inveresk than at present; this was also the case with most neighbouring settlements. In the late 1940s, there were at least seven shops which supplied hardware, haberdashery, coal, and building materials, and they included a cobbler, a butcher, a baker and grocer. Older people also recall that both bars and shops offered for sale a more extensive range of commodities even as recently as the 1960s when, of course, there were far fewer households than now with private vehicles. If people wished to shop in Westport or Foxtown, they had to travel by bus, and fewer residents at that time worked in waged employment outside Inveresk. In other words, there was greater demand for locally provisioned goods. It was also the case that businessmen and businesswomen were able to access commodities from a larger number of suppliers who were involved in tight competition between themselves.

The situation nowadays is quite different because, whilst a number of pier households are still without private cars, most residents are able to acquire their domestic requirements each week from supermarkets in either Foxtown or Westport. In the two market towns are concentrated the retail outlets which are part of commercial conglomerates dominating the country as a whole. Smaller enterprises have little chance of competing with them, hence the high turnover of stores in both towns which try to do so. The current situation is also different in that the number of wholesalers supplying smaller country establishments has shrunk. Within a rural locality like that surrounding Inveresk, the same supplier often now provides all the stores or all the public houses with the same commodity range.

The end result is a high degree of competitiveness over minimal profits at the periphery. The mean-spirited attitude of village entrepreneurs, their 'money mindedness' in folk terminology, is at least in substantial part the inevitable, localised outcome of these wider market and institutional forces. Businessmen and women have little choice but to be acutely concerned with minor profit margins, not least because the lessons of failing to do so are evident enough. By the late 1980s and early 1990s, the high streets of both market towns displayed a considerable number of vacated shops, whilst within Inveresk itself, one pier shop to all intents and purposes had ceased trading by late 1993, and the other (which was owned by the Scully family) was rented out to a pier housewife gamely trying to wrest a profit from summer trade alone. I have already mentioned that by that year too one village bar opened only at weekends and attracted little custom. Subsequent to my fieldwork, it was managed by an inexperienced young couple from outside the community who lasted only a few months before it was sold on again to a prosperous businessman, also from outside, who intended to modernise it. This he duly did, but only to sell it on yet again. For all those who remained in business by the early 1990s and later, building and retaining a regular clientele continued to be highly problematic.

BUYERS AND BAILIFFS

The way in which the pier is articulated into the wider political economy is especially involved. This is somewhat paradoxical because, by contrast with the sustained historical role of the state in the reform of agriculture, fishing has received no such attention. Neither before joining the Common Market nor in the years after it was this industry considered important enough for structural reform or major investment by the state. The number of men employed in the fishing industry has always been a small percentage of the country's labour force, the contribution to gross national product has been slight, and the highly dispersed character of the industry has stood in the way of strong political representation in a system where regional bloc votes are essential if an economic issue is to be properly addressed.

In Inveresk's port, therefore, there is minimal evidence of intervention by the state. Only one boat has been built for a local fisherman by Bord Iascaigh Mhara (the Sea Fisheries' Board), the breakwater is crumbling into the sea, the harbour is dredged only rarely, and there is little by way of grants for purchasing boats or fishing gear. What local people fish with is what they have come to possess through their own efforts over the years. Moreover, precisely because this is small-scale fishing with all the uncertainties and insecurities that this entails, any kind of bank loan for the upgrading of vessels or gear is extremely hard to come by.

The most important dimension of external articulation concerns the sale of fish in the national and international marketplaces. This is not done by a major institutional body, on the lines of the farmers' prosperous cooperative, but by individuals involved in high risk trading, the effects of which rebound throughout the pier domain. The central figure here is the fish dealer who buys directly from the boats, and then sells through personal trading networks as far afield as the fish markets of Dublin, Manchester, London and Paris. There are always two, and often enough three, men inside the community who fill this role, and they are involved in intense competition between themselves for a regular, diverse supply of fish throughout the year. Sometimes even this competition is compounded by non-local entrepreneurs trading on their own account or buying for foreign fish processing firms, but their incursions are not likely to last long.

There is no contractual relationship between a fish dealer and a boat's owner-skipper. The prices on offer from each buyer for different types of

36 A WORLD OF FINE DIFFERENCE

fish are public knowledge because of the efficiency of bar talk, so each skipper sells his catch for the best price he can get. But there are two qualifications to this. First, the sale of fish is always done on credit: the owner does not receive payment until the end of the week; in the interim the dealer can run into unforeseen problems, and these can impact on all his local suppliers. The second qualification is more involved. If a boat is fishing particularly well, the buyer may raise all his prices for that owner in order to encourage him to maintain regular supply. Alternatively, if he requires the steady supply of a particular kind of fish (salmon, for instance), he may offer the skipper a good price in advance in order to consolidate the arrangement between them. Once another buyer gets wind of such arrangements, however, he has no compunction about making a better offer for the catch of a successful boat, in other words of poaching his competitor's trade. Each buyer is constantly on the lookout for new supplies and the tactics adopted can be fairly rough.

One tactic is to encourage speculation that a rival is becoming increasingly unreliable because of a shortage of cash, a rumour which can be effective since this does occur quite often. It arises because no buyer is able to make a livelihood from trading in fish from Inveresk alone: each has to cultivate skippers in other ports along the coast, as well as to buy on the auction floor of fishing cooperatives in the region. Then again, as well as having several sources of supply, a fish dealer has to sell through multiple outlets, ranging from fish sellers in nearby towns whom he knows well, through to merchants further afield whom he may never have met and communicates with simply by phone. The problem is that as the dealer works to maximise his trading position, there is a constant danger of his becoming overextended capital-wise; and however skilful he might be, his calculations can always be bowled over by another dealer defaulting on major payments, for all this regional trade is conducted on credit terms too.

The local upshot of this is that the dealer fails, in part or in whole, to pay his skippers in Inveresk as previously agreed. The skipper cannot cover his costs, his sharemen are without cash in hand for at least a week, and the result is conflict between all concerned. If substantial sums are involved, this takes the form of open dispute. Throughout the 1980s, the leading buyer was Johnny Dawson, a blow-in who conducted all his trade from the somewhat dilapidated house which many considered to demarcate the boundary between village and pier. Before entering the fish trade, Dawson had been a bookie constantly on the move between horse and dog racing tracks in England and Ireland, a business which he considered sound training for a fish merchant: 'We're all fucking gangsters in this trade', he once told me, 'and if you're not a fucking gangster, you won't survive five minutes'. He expended a lot of energy cultivating his relations with boat owners, but from time to time he was threatened with a beating from bellicose skippers and sharemen to whom he owed considerable sums of money.

Relations between a buyer and his skippers can be most amicable. When fish prices are high and supply is steady, an enterprising buyer like Dawson can bring high cash returns to the pier, whereupon the bars become lively places. But when cheques begin to bounce or payments are indefinitely delayed, the atmosphere rapidly changes to one of acrimony. At such times the prospect of establishing a fish cooperative is mooted, for other communities along the coast have developed well-organised cooperatives. They are not without problems, but at least they have offset some of the uncertainties which proliferate in small scale fishing. Before long, however, in Inveresk this public conversation falters and then peters out. Interpersonal and interfamilial jealousies at the pier are considered too substantial an obstacle for the necessary organisational momentum to be generated.

What impact the state does have on fishing is predominantly negative, especially during the summer salmon season. This is the time of year when Inveresk fisherman can, as they put it, 'make some serious money', that is realise a return well in excess of recurrent financial commitments. From the proceeds, they can finance house improvements, acquire new gear, repair big boats, or purchase a new punt. For this reason, the season is approached with enthusiasm and many economic and social adjustments are made in advance.[5] However, fishing for salmon is by no means straightforward. The state specifies the type of net, net size and length, the duration of the season, the times fishing is permitted during the week, and specific rules cover both punt and big boat fishing. But if there is no other type of fishing which is so rule regulated, nor is there one where regulations are so roundly flouted, and this is because fishermen need to maximise on the opportunities which the salmon holds out.

One major result of salmon fishing being so profitable is heightened tension between the fishermen themselves. Since the best sites for inshore fishing are limited, overcrowding occurs regularly and disputes break out. A full string of monofilament nets may be over two miles long, so that one net is often cast inadvertently over another, or powerful tides tangle them together, or they get entangled with the buoys and lines marking lobster pots. The result is conflict between skippers and between boats, all of which is heightened by the fact that the salmon is locally considered the ultimate test of fishing skill.

On the other hand, what sometimes holds these tensions in check is the need to cooperate against the bailiffs, officers employed by the regional fisheries' board. Even coastal communities which traditionally

A WORLD OF FINE DIFFERENCE

have little to do with one another cooperate against these much-disliked state officials. As soon as their high-powered boats are seen either in the vicinity of communities like Inveresk or out to sea, the information is passed on either over CB radio or the public phones installed in fishermen's bars. Whenever the message comes through that a bailiffs' raid is pending, fishermen work together to clear the bay of illegal nets as quickly as possible. Out at sea, when a big boat is pitted against that of the bailiffs, others will go to its assistance, so when, after the close of the 1988 season, Tommy McCarthy was caught with a salmon string only half-hauled, he was aided by Dickie Geoghagen who circled the sole bailiffs' vessel with his own, trailing in the water two heavy ropes in order to foul the bailiffs' propeller. Outnumbered and outmanoeuvred, the latter beat a hasty retreat.

Incidents such as this are the essence of narratives which accentuate and celebrate the distinctive properties of pier experience, so more will be said about them subsequently. Here the point is that the extremes of close cooperation and intense conflict at the pier are substantially compounded by the way the fishing industry is related to the wider political economy. The state has allowed the mechanisms of the marketplace to prevail in the industry as a whole. In the peripheral context of Inveresk, the main result is that the instabilities of this trade in highly perishable commodities are concentrated in the hands of the independent buyer, and this generates further tensions and conflicts throughout the pier domain. The only visible part played by the state is a policing role, and whilst this assuredly makes all the more important cooperation between fishermen, it produces some of the most striking conflicts involving pier people.

THE DISCOURSE OF DOMAINS

I have argued that the cultural differences between Inveresk's three domains – reserve and restraint among country folk, sociability and competition in the village, camaraderie and conflict amongst pier people – are to be understood by reference to the contrasting means of livelihood which predominate in each domain, and their relation to the wider political economy in which the community is inextricably embedded.

Several important consequences flow from these contrasts, the first of which is that the natural discourse which prevails in each place is quite different from the other two. By discourse I refer here to the habitual speech acts and the recurrent conversational subject matters which are prevalent in each domain on a daily basis.[6] This definition incorporates the recurrent subjects thrown up by the elementary tasks of making a living, the familial concerns which inhabitants consider of pressing

REGIONAL RELATIONS AND LOCAL IDENTITIES

consequence, and the personal issues which people address in talk, all of which have to be dealt with in ways which are considered locally appropriate and conventional. This is not a matter of people being conservative: it is a question of economy for so much of this discourse is integrated into the routines of making one's livelihood, and is integral to making sense of it as it customarily unfolds.

Each place-specific discourse reflects first and foremost the predominant economic concerns of pier, country or village, as well as the social relations which arise from them. So there is, as one might anticipate, constant talk about the details of crops and animals in the country, the availability of different types of fish amongst pier folk, and in the village the difficulties of how to conduct a business enterprise in an adverse economic climate. As one might also expect, at least in the pier and the country there is an habitual concern with the weather as well as commodity prices. Weather conditions are a matter of vital importance to farmers and fishermen alike, and so all forecasts on television and radio are monitored. As already explained, the small scale of fishing out of Inveresk ensures it is highly susceptible to even minor changes in weather conditions, and so close attention is paid to the judgement of two older, retired fishermen who, by general agreement, are most adept at predicting local conditions over the next few hours or couple of days.

A good deal of fishing discourse is necessarily about changes in the prices on offer from local and non-local buyers, as well as the constant tribulations of dealing with them. Although most commodity prices for farmers are slow changing or allow no alternatives, all farmers with animals to sell have to keep an eye on the state of play in the cattle and sheep market at Westport, and on the prices being offered by dealers working for the major meat trading companies in the region. No young or middle-aged farmer, however, has the time to make a weekly visit to the mart, as it is called, so they rely on conversations (first-hand or otherwise) with a couple of older tillage farmers who buy in calves and feed them up over eighteen months for eventual resale. They are bachelor countrymen with time on their hands to attend the mart regularly, and their judgement on price trends is considered absolutely sound.

Likewise prominent in place-specific discourses are the technological considerations most pressing for farmers and fishermen alike. Those in both occupations are generally adept at the maintenance and repair of their equipment: besides this being of economic importance (any kind of major repair work is an expensive exercise in this peripheral setting), men are judged according to their mechanical skills. To be considered 'handless' is to be damned as near-useless in a setting like this where, at the least, any man should be able to service his own vehicles, his agricultural

40 A WORLD OF FINE DIFFERENCE

equipment, or the engine on his boat. This is one area where farmers do cooperate with their neighbours from time to time, even though equipment is only shared with close relatives. At the pier, scarcely a day passes without two or three boat owners publicly working away at a faulty engine or net hauler.

There are limits to what can be done through pooling local expertise, so that some measure of domain discourse revolves around the respective qualities of the few men in the region who make their livelihoods from itinerant, mechanical repair work. How good each is must be closely scrutinised since no self-employed person is going to put valuable equipment in the hands of an ill-disciplined mechanic. Charlie Foley's repair work on boat engines is constantly reviewed because, whilst he is considered an especially skilled mechanic, this Foxtown resident has a drinking problem which can make him unreliable. Seemingly endless talk revolves around whether the latter quality cancels out the former, and whether his especially current knowledge about fishing in the region figures in the equation at all.

It is, however, the state of parochial social relations as these bear on economic interests which pervades domain discourse, for it is recognised, especially in the village and at the pier, that ongoing interpersonal relations are a significant determinant of material success. Despite the regular competition and the occasional hostilities which keep them apart, shop owners and publicans are well aware of how everyone else is faring. They closely monitor talk about the relations which their rivals have with their respective clienteles, and they go to considerable lengths to win over local custom on the strength of it. The results of this can be involved. I have already mentioned the difficulties facing Conor Neeson's village bar by the early 1990s. I frequently heard it argued that the root problem was that the owner had come to rely too heavily on a small and declining clique of older customers, and quite failed to monitor the improvements which competitors had been making. Some of these had been in response to a proliferation of sports groups in the community, so that presentation nights following weekend-long competitions had become a lucrative source of income for public house owners.

Keeping abreast of the social relations which palpably affect economic performance is exemplified by the specifics of day-to-day discourse at the pier. Once a boat pulls out of the harbour around 7.00 to 7.30 in the morning and basic tasks are out of the way, a crew will casually pool the range of information which they have variously gleaned from bar conversations and street talk on the previous night, and all this is assimilated by a skipper to inform decisions which he will take during the course of the day. It is by no means unusual for a skipper to change

REGIONAL RELATIONS AND LOCAL IDENTITIES 41

tactics for the entire day on the basis of these details about the location of other boats, how well each has been doing, whether bailiffs are rumoured to be around, as well as the prices on offer from buyers other than his current associate. Crew members do not see this last minute decision making as a sign of indecisiveness. They would be unimpressed if the skipper appeared so fixed in his own judgement that he did not respond to their inputs.

So the natural discourse of each domain comprises the condensed, coherent, and collective conversation which draws on, and adds to, the ever-changing stock of knowledge shared by those involved in its prevalent means of livelihood. This is not an evenly distributed body of knowledge: certain residents are adept at keeping valuable information to themselves, and it is part of their local reputations that they do so. Knowledge may not be interchangeable with power in this small-scale setting,[7] but it is undoubtedly a valuable resource and has to be marshalled accordingly. Nor should it be concluded that these place-specific ways of talking necessarily exclude those not involved in the domain's prevalent occupation. At this point it warrants repetition that the country, the village and the pier are all internally heterogeneous places, especially in occupational terms. Yet the women and the men who are in other kinds of work (or do not work at all) have generally lived alongside either farmers, or fishermen, or business folk for much of their lives, and they are often connected with them through kinship or friendship. Under these circumstances, it is clearly improbable that these local discourses have the capacity to entirely exclude others in the way that, for example, ethnic discourses do in segregated urban locales.

The situation is instead one of degree, for whilst it is certainly the case that a country resident who is not of farm stock may be able to follow much of the work-related conversation between two or three farmers, the detail and the depth of many such exchanges make it unlikely that the former's appreciation will be on the same plane as the main speaking partners. The effect of such exchanges is not the total exclusion which often results from interethnic verbal encounters, but instead one of discomforting marginalisation, a sense of being merely present at a conversation rather than a party to it, a feeling of not being able to grasp the full significance of what others evidently share.

My experience is this respect was salutary. In my first year of fieldwork, in the course of conducting a detailed survey of all farms in the townland, I came to know all farm household heads; and since I talked with some several times, my knowledge of agricultural matters increased quite rapidly (or so I thought). In order to consolidate this, I took every advantage of being resident on the boundary between country and

42   A WORLD OF FINE DIFFERENCE

village. Quite conscientiously, I became a regular customer at the farmers' house, the one place in the village where farmers are able to talk with one another at ease and at length. Yet even after a year's residence, I found it difficult to follow lengthy conversations unless they concerned topics on which I had specifically focused in talk with them.

This was not, perhaps, entirely my own ineptitude coming to the fore. At the other end of the community, one of the most astute observers of Inveresk life from within was a university-educated secondary school teacher in his late thirties, who originated from a community (in the same county) not all that different from Inveresk, and who had married into one of its best known village families over a decade previously. An active member of community associations, he was a regular drinker at a pier bar where he was accepted by most fishermen and appeared at ease in their company. Yet on one occasion when we were conversing at his home, Colm reflected: 'Although I know them all right and have for years, I'll lose track when they're talking to one another all the time. I'll be standing there, I'll miss something, and I'll be right out of it.' He went on to say: 'If I'm not in on a conversation from the start, I'll easily get left behind. It's a waste of time trying to catch up, so I'll just wander off, like, and play some cards or some dominoes.'

SENSE OF PLACE, SENSE OF IDENTITY

One reason why this qualified sense of marginality is common among blow-ins like Colm Higgins is that they are often employed outside the community, and this necessarily puts them at a further step removed from many of the incidents which are incorporated into the discursive currents of everyday life. But an equally important factor is that so much of these place-specific discourses implicates the ramified and fully fledged identities which long-term residents have acquired and modified, con-structed and reconstructed, over their lifetimes in Inveresk. The complexity of these identities is not easily comprehended, especially when conversation referring to them is more often implicit than explicit. On the other hand, where that complexity is properly apprehended in the routine flow of domain-specific talk, there can be no experience more generative of the feeling that this place is the one to which one naturally belongs.

Because the majority of Inveresk folk have been born, and have matured in or near to, the specific places where they currently reside, so their social identities are inextricably associated with the distinctive web of relations constituted over time in the village, at the pier, or in the country. To summarise thus far: each domain occupies a distinct space on the physical landscape; it is distinguished by a particular means of realising a

REGIONAL RELATIONS AND LOCAL IDENTITIES 43

livelihood; it is characterised by distinct codes of interpersonal conduct; and it is, as we have just seen, marked by its specific natural discourse as well. In these circumstances, the linkage between who one is and the domain to which one belongs is especially close, even to the point of being inseparable. Inveresk residents well recognise they are products of these particular milieux, that their identities are as much visited on them by socially proximate others as by any other consideration, including their own choice or volition.

There are two elements to this, the way in which individuals are implicated in the identities socially associated with their families, and the way personal attributes have become attached to them by their peers over time. The first consideration, essentially, is that the individual's identity is on the whole inseparable from that of the family into which he or she was born. Over time, families have become typified according to the prevalent standards of pier, country and village behaviour; this socially constructed family identity becomes part of the individual's identity as well. Across Inveresk's rural hinterland, for example, the Carty family is considered 'pure country' in the way it conducts itself. Fintan and Ellen Carty, who are middle aged and have two older children in wage-employment, live in a fine two-storey house in a narrow valley which is only about four kilometres from the village. Fintan runs single-handedly the 106-acre dairy farm which he has fully modernised. He rarely leaves the farm during an average week, his wife visits the village only occasionally, and she has little to do with her neighbours: 'I'll talk to them nicely if I run into them outside the church, but being farming people we're not all that bothered about that neighbourly business.' The parents' social life is effectively restricted to visiting close relatives who live at some distance from the area and are all farming people. Without demur, the Cartys proudly describe themselves as 'respectable people who keep ourselves to ourselves'. This is also how they are seen by their neighbours: in their eyes too, the Cartys are quintessential country folk.

At the other end of Inveresk, members of the Brown family are considered archetypal pier people. They live in a small bungalow which is owned by the family's matriarch who has two daughters and six sons. This household is always full of people and it is dominated by talk about fish since all the sons and the husbands of both daughters are full-time or part-time fishermen. Three, sometimes four, of the sons live at home either out of preference or because they cannot afford to rent accommodation for their young families. None of them, despite all being considered good fishermen, owns a big boat, and this is because, so it is said, a wasteful or feckless streak runs throughout the family. What is indisputable is that

44 A WORLD OF FINE DIFFERENCE

the Browns are 'pure pier' in combining intense family loyalty with undisguised attachment to this specific place. Their fortunes are inseparable from those of the McGarrity family who live alongside them, who fish with their menfolk, and with whom they have intermarried; the eldest of the Brown daughters is married to the eldest of four McGarrity brothers. These relations are pivotal at the pier because together the families are a potent political force.[8] This is also why both families are considered pier people without equal: whilst exemplifying the camaraderie expected of pier residents, they are recurrently at the centre of some of its more damaging disputes.

So certain families are considered to epitomise the qualities prevalent in their domain of residence, and these qualities are integral to their own felt identity. Just as the Cartys confidently pronounce themselves 'respectable country folk', the Browns are proud of the down-to-earth and uncomplicated way in which they order their affairs. Although I never heard them put it this way, their self-image is that of being 'salt of the earth'. The corollary of this is that other families are characterised according to how much they deviate, so to speak, from these standards of typified conduct. One example has already been mentioned in the previous chapter: Peadar and Nuala O'Donnell who own the farmers' house are assuredly village people on many counts, but in temperament and style it is widely said that 'they have a bit of country in them'. One of the justifications for this observation is that they are concerned to keep 'a respectable (public) house' from which it possible to get ejected for unruly behaviour. Anyone who is thoroughly inebriated or whose language gets excessively crude won't get served. Peadar – 'a real gentleman married to a real lady', as one farmer expressed it – is often compared to his brother Seamus whose own bar in the village can get very unruly indeed, and this is because he and his wife are 'altogether money minded'. To quote the same farmer: 'Provided you've got the cash in your pocket, Seamus'll keep serving you pints whatever the state you're in'. In other words, this branch of the O'Donnell family is about as 'village' in calibre as it is possible to be.

Inveresk residents take enormous satisfaction in exploring fine differences like these because the qualities associated with these extended families are considered to be 'in the blood'. It is assumed that they will be somehow shared by all family members, and individual personalities are closely scrutinised to establish the presence (or otherwise) of such inherited traits. When, for example, a son in a farm family fails to display interest in following in his father's footsteps, that is he does not exhibit the same profound attachment to the land and everything that grows or walks on it, this is put down to its not being 'in his blood' for some reason or other. Alternatively, some pier families are not only considered to have 'rough' qualities which are 'in their blood', but this 'roughness' can also run to excess – what people refer to as 'bad blood' – which provides an explanation for their having an especially foul tongue or being prone to acts of violence.

A family reputation of this type can be an exceptional burden. Along with another shareman, I once became involved in a sustained drinking session with Éamon McGarrity who was at the time widely considered 'a real blackguard' because of 'the bad blood coming out in him' (he was 20 at the time), as were the two first cousins to whom he was close. Beginning at the pier, working through the village, and ending up about midnight at Máire Neeson's Night Club, the drink had taken its toll, but Éamon was in the mood for some powerful reflection: 'This is a shit place to live, boy, and I'm going to get the fuck out of it. If you're a McGarrity in this hole, there's always some fucker waiting to hang you. As soon as you put a foot wrong, if you're a McGarrity they'll fucking hang you – and they'll hang you high.'

The identity of the individual thus refracts the domain-specific identity of the family into which he or she was born. More particular still is the recognition of consistent and complementary individual traits and qualities which similarly get singled out for special mention. Since the long-term residents of each domain have grown up together, they have passed through its rituals in concert, they have shared major successes and failures, as well as – in not a few cases – exceptional tragedy. In these circumstances, the individual's developing temperament and emergent character have always been open to public view, to the extent that much of his or her behaviour is now predictable and explicable. So when even a relatively inconsequential incident transpires, precedent will frequently be found for it. When, for example, a shareman in a fit of pique threw overboard some old but serviceable gear after an especially miserable and unproductive winter's day at sea, the response was: 'Sure the man has always been like that, wasn't he just like that when we were all in the (National) school together?'

Alternatively, the explanation for particular actions will be discovered in the individual's specific history. Inveresk has several residents considered to have serious drinking problems, and some are considered psychologically disturbed. In a few instances, their difficulties are put down to its 'being in the blood', but in rather more it is linked to something like a tragic moment in the past which left an indelible influence on personality development. One middle-aged man, who for many years has lived apart from his wife and whose alcohol-driven excesses alternately amuse and horrify, is endlessly tolerated because his infant child was killed in a freak

46 A WORLD OF FINE DIFFERENCE

accident. Whenever a visitor comments adversely on his behaviour, he or she will always be firmly told what a fine and upstanding fellow he had been prior to the tragedy.

This kind of attribution, though, is not restricted to the few. In the concentrated fields of pier, country and village, individual identities are constantly subject to evaluation and revaluation, constitution and reconstitution, and in these intricately fashioned accounts is distilled a wealth of past experience and contemporary observation. Some indication of this is found in the distribution of nicknames at the pier where, as we have seen, social intimacy is most pronounced.[9] John Brown, for example, is usually referred to as Floss because physically and personality-wise he bears a strong resemblance to his long-deceased father. Floss was his father's nickname, so now its usage honours 'the blood' which has flowed between the two generations. John's brother Tadgh bears the nickname the Cat because of his remarkable agility when at sea. Whilst others struggle to move around vessels filled to the gills with monofilament nets and other gear, the Cat is amazingly adept, moving especially fast to gaff a salmon which is about to slip the net. And then there are other nicknames like Scan, Swannee, Brasso, Twig, the Bee, Starch, Monk, and Hammer, most of which have some particular historical or social connotation for the individuals who own or deploy them, (whilst in the country where maintaining social distance is the order of the day, not a single farmer bears a recognised nickname).

IDENTITY AND BELONGING

Evidence of the impact of exogenous economic and political forces is, as we have seen, as marked on the landscape of Inveresk as it is on any other community in modern Ireland. But it is equally true that this is a social world which its established residents have constructed and continue to construct for themselves as members of families and as individuals. The typical farm property in the country is a site of additions and improvements over (at least) two or three earlier generations, and this is a pattern which the current farm family continues to take further. In the village, public houses especially bear the physical hallmarks of their past and current owners, whilst the prevalent ambience of each reflects the character of the incumbent publican, the man who is expected to be fully in charge. At the pier, boats which were inherited from the older generation, *Free State* for example, clearly display the physical marks of prior ownership, but these are now compounded by more recent innovations: not even the mechanical net hauler is the same on any two vessels, and this is because each skipper works his boat differently.

Above all, however, it is the content and the composition of social relations in each specific place that express most clearly the extent to which this is a peripheral world of its residents' own making. At the core of this process is its singular, natural discourse, the resource with which people compare the experiences of being a full member of one domain with what is known about domain membership elsewhere. In each of these, select families are held to personify the qualities distinctive to, and most highly regarded by, others: even when deviations or exceptions can be found, they are explained away in a fashion which reinforces prevalent stereotypes. Most important, it is within the specific places of country, village, and pier that the individual is recognised and related to as a fully rounded, complete, and complex social persona. It may well be that a farmer and a fisherman have known each other for three, four or more decades in Inveresk. But such is the difference between them in social terms that neither can claim true familiarity with the other. There is, in fact, just one close friendship between a farmer and a fisherman which has endured for over four decades; what is most telling about this relation is precisely that it is recognised as an exceptional bond by all concerned, including the men themselves. The dominant pattern is for long-standing residents to have their close kin, their close friends, and therefore the most important activities which are rooted in these relations, concentrated within their domain of origin. From the individual's vantage point, this microcosm is his or her paramount reality, the social world in which the influence of family background and his or her own idiosyncratic qualities, are recognised and appreciated. The pier, country, or village is where the individual qua individual is fully, expansively known.

It follows from these considerations that it is precisely in the everyday elaboration of domain-specific discourse that the essence of belonging is constituted and experienced. It is in the ability to contribute naturally and effortlessly to the talk in which the details and intricacies of domain activity are distilled that the sense of being fully at home can be realised. It is in this fashion that the individual comes to experience, in Richardson's words, 'the social well-being attached to the sense of rootedness in place' (1984: 66).[10] Whilst the blow-in as recent incomer might feel marginalised by a discourse which unfolds in front of him or her but with which it is not possible to connect effectively, the long-established resident experiences all the satisfaction of profound familiarity. This is not simply a matter of understanding the specifics of what others like oneself are saying, but also of experiencing the unrivalled sense of taking one's proper place in the world, of being amongst those with whom one has the greatest affinity.

48   A WORLD OF FINE DIFFERENCE

In the course of all this, it must be remembered that only a minority of residents do not have contact with those from immediately proximate domains on a fairly regular basis. In the course of a day or two, a village resident will customarily encounter country and pier residents. In the course of a week, most pier people will run across and talk with several villagers; and over a month or two, a country resident will likely converse, however briefly, with someone from the pier either on the street, in the village, or outside the church. But such are the marked differences between Inveresk folk that these encounters are as likely to underscore that one is essentially a villager, a countryman, or 'true pier' as having any other outcome. This is the real significance of their juxtaposition. Precisely because residents do regularly move and frequently interact across the boundaries between domains, the experience serves to confirm that there is only one specific place in the community to which their sense of individual attachment is quite without qualification.

4

DIFFERENCE AND DISPUTE

It will be evident that any attempt to present Inveresk to the outside world as a unified community will be difficult. At the least, any individual or group which takes on this goal is going to have to be sensitive to the cultural differences between its domains. The task is made all the more problematic by considerations of family loyalty and prestige. Indeed, in certain respects the differences which exist between prominent families are more difficult to come to terms with because, whilst there is no prospect of domain memberships acting corporately, influential families do precisely this from time to time, on occasion with major impact on the broader social fabric. It should be clear by now, however, that the general differences between domains and the specific relations between families inside them are different sides of the same coin. How families relate to one another is very much constitutive of how each domain differs from the other two.

The concern of this chapter is to examine how social differentiation between families articulates with differences between pier, village and country, to consider in other words how the social organisation of families compounds the different senses of place experienced within the community. This entails addressing also the extent to which Inveresk lives up to its reputation as a tough little settlement. As indicated in chapter 1, the inhabitants of neighbouring communities who are familiar with Inveresk frequently characterise it in negative terms: they consider it a clannish and conflict-ridden place whose inhabitants are obsessed with one another to an unhealthy degree. The residents themselves do not shy away from this reputation: some incline to consider it well merited; and certainly for as long as I have been living there, significant disputes have always been under way. [1]

A WORLD OF FINE DIFFERENCE

THE EXTENDED FAMILY AND ITS LOYALTIES

Families in Inveresk vary considerably. But in relation to the community's politics, the first significant quality is that as corporate groups they are often substantial; the nuclear family functioning in its own right is in the minority here. Since it was common in the previous generation to have several children, Inveresk's families typically have two, three or four branches within the community. Since patrilocality is also the norm, brothers and their dependants often reside relatively proximate to one another and interact frequently. In the country, for example, Thomas and Owen O'Duffy have farms of about 100 acres each within Inveresk townland, and a third brother with a somewhat larger acreage resides just a few miles beyond the townland. In the village, I have already detailed the co-presence of Peadar and Seamus O'Donnell, the village publicans. At the pier, not only do Barry, Stephen and Oliver McGarrity live close by one another whilst the youngest brother Lewis owns a bungalow in the village, but Barry and Stephen have fished together for several years and Oliver and Lewis occasionally do so.

The second property is that these families always include blow-in members, especially women drawn from villages and towns within a modest radius of Inveresk. Some spouses who have married in are from much further afield: women and men have travelled overseas, married in the United Kingdom or the United States, and then returned with their spouses to resume residence. But most are drawn from much closer sources and their incorporation into the community has been a protracted affair as a result. Over several months prior to marriage, they have visited the place regularly and acquired some knowledge of how it functions.

This is not to say that incorporation into a local family or the community at large was straightforward. Two women, who married into the McGarrity family from nearby villages over 15 years previously, professed themselves to be still alarmed by the happenings in which extended family members were involved. During a kitchen table conversation, one turned to the other and said: 'You've got to admit it now Nora, the McGarritys are a queer family altogether, as queer a family as you could come across anywhere. The things they get up to! I can't imagine any of that happening where I come from.' A young woman who had married into the equally prominent Hyde family complained that, although prior to marriage she had a sense of how difficult interpersonal relations could be in Inveresk, 'None of that had prepared me for what it was really like. Early on I went home to my mum and cried my eyes out because of the gossip going on about Mossie's family. It was just so mean, so vicious.' Both of these female blow-ins were from small rural communities no more than six miles distant.

DIFFERENCE AND DISPUTE 51

The third quality is the pervasive emphasis on loyalty to kinsfolk. Family loyalty is quite fundamental to the social organisation of this locale, and when a family fails to sustain its members' strong attachment, it is to be lamented. Relations between the middle-aged Barry brothers, two of whom reside in the country, the third at the pier, but all of whom are fishermen, are known to be poor. The middle-born once told me: 'I don't know why it is but somehow we just don't get on. We never have. It's as if we're not of the same blood.' At least of some relevance was a falling out over inheritable property when the eldest brother returned from the United States to find that regular remittances had not been put to his chosen purpose. In general terms though, Inveresk residents are strongly committed to the extended family and take every opportunity to express the fact publicly.

There are many of these, the most regular being visits to the bar at weekends when the different branches of some families routinely meet up and publicly affirm their cohesiveness. Alternatively, at Christmas, on St Patrick's Day or when presentations are made following important events, extended families frequently arrive as a virtual cohort and remain in one another's company for the evening. During 1993, the most conspicuous public display was undertaken by the Sweeneys, one branch of which lived at the pier, the other in the village. Their goal was to renovate an old cottage at the centre of the village which Sam Sweeney had bought from his mother's brother, and into which he proposed to move his wife and children from his father's pier bungalow. For five months, his father and his three brothers, along with his father's older brother and his eldest son, threw their collective expertise into the task. It became the family's proud boast that they could muster from their own ranks all the manual labour and building expertise required, and at the weekends all the menfolk and some of the younger wives retired to the farmers' house where Sam's father's brother's wife was employed behind the bar.

This was a striking display of family solidarity: for most, the commitment is expressed less conspicuously. What is broadly agreed is that the familial network which people refer to as 'close kin' or 'real kin' does not extend to the level of cousinhood. First cousins are not considered 'close' family members when important issues are afoot, and this is because there is not, as people express it, 'the thickness of blood there' to warrant sharing important confidences, which is where the definitive line is drawn between 'real kin' and the rest. 'Real kin' are those with whom one can be totally candid, and loyalty will ensure that the confidence will be kept. In the words of Sam Sweeney: 'You can say whatever comes into your head, you can spout off as to what's bothering you, without its getting out of the room. And you can't do that with cousins 'cos there's not the same thickness of blood there, y' know?'

Cousins are often considered so distant that the bond of friendship is more important. When I returned to the village in 1993, one of the first residents I visited was a woman in her fifties whose husband (a man I knew well) had recently died. After I had expressed my condolences, she told me how another village woman had supported her greatly during her bereavement. I knew that she was referring to her first cousin, so I commented blithely that during difficult times it was good to have relatives on hand. She put me straight: 'Ah no, that's not important at all, she's just always been my dear friend down over the years'. One of the reasons for drawing the line so emphatically between 'close kin' and cousins is that, as a result of extensive intermarriage locally, some residents can identify eight or ten cousins, but they would not welcome being associated with some of them.

Status considerations often lie behind such attempts at social distancing. More significantly, they can compound historical tensions between families as well as influence contemporary disputes over land or buildings. Inveresk residents can become acutely concerned with status differences, and some take major offence at the slights detectable in otherwise innocuous incidents. The claims repeatedly made to strangers are that 'we're all much the same round here', 'you'll find no really rich and no really poor, we're much of a muchness really', and 'there are no classes around here, we're all much the same'. But these claims to equality are often a façade behind which status considerations are pursued with vigour, and when this happens, it is the petit bourgeois rank of residents which give the resultant tensions an exaggerated, sometimes destructive, quality.

The relevant point is that, whilst it can be superficially proclaimed that 'everyone here is his own man' and that 'everyone hereabouts is as good as his neighbour', when examined closely and matched with sequences of interaction these oft-made claims to strict egalitarianism can prove misleading. The status which comes from being in private ownership of productive property is more justified and assured for some than for others. It is true that the farmer who owns 70 acres of land and the fisherman who owns a 35 foot boat are similarly in possession of productive property, and on that criterion alone can be constructed a semblance of equality. But whilst the land is always the farmer's sole source of livelihood, the fisherman typically requires state support in the form of dole payments for some part of the year. Whilst the publican owns his public house and accommodation incorporated into it, and the fisherman owns his own punt, there may be as much, if not more, to differentiate between them than what renders them socially equal.

The claim to equality is genuinely articulated by many residents and it assuredly informs a great deal of face-to-face interaction. But below the

DIFFERENCE AND DISPUTE 53

surface, the situation can be very different so that one quite often, but always in private contexts, encounters the judgement that pier people are generally low class whilst those in the village and country are generally middle class. This is only in part to do with class in the narrow sense of productive property ownership: it is cast as well in terms of prevalent lifestyle, with the emphasis on pier folk occupying council houses (in several cases mobile homes), using rougher speech forms, spending time and money in bars, being less concerned with children's education, and being inclined to disreputable behaviour (extra-marital affairs for example). These distinctly localised judgements of class are rarely articulated in public, and even when expressed in private they are qualified: 'I don't want to sound like a shilling looking down on a penny, but . . .'. When they do surface, however, they are strongly responded to, especially when they get bound up with expressions of family loyalty.

FAMILIES IN DISPUTE

One empirical example can only illustrate some of these concerns, but a case in point emerged in early 1988. It eventually dominated much of domain-specific discourse at the pier where most, but significantly not all, of the protagonists were resident. In the first instance, the central figure was Mickey Brown, the youngest of six sons in the prominent pier family encountered in chapter 3. Pier opinion was that Mickey was considerably more reliable than some of his elder brothers. In his early twenties, he was a shareman on Kevin Coogan's boat, one of the best equipped and maintained vessels. The skipper too was in his early twenties, although not from a fishing family. His father Liam had a mixed career, including running his own contracting business, until he had been bought out by a national corporation.

With some of this capital, he established his son as a boat owner. Liam's wife was rumoured to have been firmly against this: born into a local farm family whose members emphatically considered themselves middle class, Elizabeth had hoped that her son would pursue a more respectable career. Part of the business arrangement was that Liam would assume responsibility for selling his son's catch, thus keeping a close eye on the operation. This division of labour worked well, but Liam never missed an opportunity to broadcast loudly his son's achievements, much to the irritation of other fishermen.

Mickey and Kevin fished effectively together until Mickey began to court the elder of Liam and Elizabeth's daughters. Initially this generated little comment, but as the relationship flourished, Dervla's parents voiced their disapproval, she duly transmitted this to Mickey, and the bond

54 A WORLD OF FINE DIFFERENCE

between them strengthened. Then Liam took a firmer line: unless the relationship ceased, Mickey would lose his berth on Kevin's boat. Mickey duly arrived at the pier one morning to be told that he was fired.

He had no difficulty in finding another berth. But across the pier domain, the incident instantly became the focus of much domain talk. General opinion was that the Coogans' behaviour was outrageous, and the Brown family was especially vocal. As one of Mickey's sisters commented: 'So they don't think our brother is good enough for their Dervla! We'll show them what the Browns are good for, and we'll start by reminding everybody about what happened when Liam married Elizabeth.' Elizabeth was from a farming background, but her mother had been renowned even by country standards for her concern with propriety and respectability. She had been strongly against (as she saw it) her daughter's marrying downwards, and the family had been riven by dispute. The current situation therefore appeared to be not all that dissimilar from that which had transpired many years previously, and the Brown family made much of the parallel.

The next step was considered even more astonishing. Liam presented his daughter with an ultimatum: she had a fortnight in which to end the relationship or move out of the family home. Dervla was considered to have inherited the personality of her headstrong father. As if to prove the point, she immediately packed her bags and moved into the already overcrowded Brown household, and for a couple of months interest subsided, until several developments took place. Liam sent a message to his daughter berating her lack of family loyalty. Then it was rumoured that Dervla's personal items were being disposed of. When she waited for Mickey at the pier, her father and brother refused to acknowledge her presence. To avoid any face-to-face encounter, Liam and Elizabeth ceased drinking in the pier bar where they had routinely met up with relatives and friends, retiring instead to the disreputable Night Club. When one of Liam's nieces was married, he and his wife failed to attend because they knew their daughter was to be a bridesmaid.

Throughout this period the Brown family was involved in a second, more serious dispute (of which more later), and the tensions generated by the one fed into the other, not least out at sea. The most public incident, though, took place in a village bar one Saturday afternoon in summer. Dervla, Mickey and two of his brothers became involved in an argument with Joseph Barry who was, by that time, openly aligned with the opposing camp to the Browns in the second dispute. In the course of some heavy banter, Mickey intimated that Joseph had been responsible recently for sinking his brother's punt. Joseph is not nicknamed the Gunner without good reason: when he proposed Mickey might repeat the accusation outside, he moved forward to give him a hand.

DIFFERENCE AND DISPUTE 55

The bar was full, the resulting chaos substantial, and when in the mêlée Dervla hit Joseph from behind, he – thinking it was one of Mickey's brothers – lashed out and connected. The bar emptied onto the street, Joseph tried to apologise, but a now-bruised Dervla berated him further. Later Joseph determined to explain to Liam, who was older than himself and for whom he had considerable respect, what had happened. When he apologetically did so, Liam's reaction was surprising but unqualified: his daughter had received her just deserts for throwing her cap in with the likes of the Brown family; Joseph should go home and forget about the whole business. Instead, now fully exonerated, Joseph fed Liam's response into bar room talk in the village, from whence it became common knowledge within hours.

FAMILIES IN THEIR DOMAINS

The first point to note is that happenings of this order are not especially unusual in Inveresk. The sources of tension and the factors that escalate them are particular. But in this restricted arena of intense face-to-face relations where these distinctly petit bourgeois matters of prestige, status and loyalty are all closely attended to, developments such as these often surface. The standing of individuals and the prestige of families are sensitive concerns, and they are exacerbated when the façade of social equality is conspicuously breached and someone publicly claims superior standing to the rest. At the best of times, such a claim is going to be hazardous, for in this setting everyone has an Achilles' heel which will be unerringly targeted. Inveresk folk frequently use the metaphor of crabs in a bucket: the closer one crab climbs to the lip, the more enthusiastically will others pull it down. Whilst the end result might be deplored, it can be put down to human nature; '. . . it's a natural kind of thing to do'.

The second point is that the lines of conflict were quickly drawn up, and in such a way as to provoke a good deal of interest not just in the pier but the village too. The Brown family have already been encountered in their role as quintessential pier people, living and working alongside one another, intimately connected through marriage and friendship with at least one other prominent family. Because of their poverty in the previous generation, and well before that, they were proud of what they had achieved in recent times, and they were sensitive to the charge that they were unpredictable and unreliable. Under the circumstances, the suggestion made so very publicly that one of their number was 'not good enough for a Coogan' was especially offensive to the Browns. Equally important in influencing popular opinion at the pier, it was a class-ridden slight which instantly raised the hackles of other domain residents.

The Coogans had their supporters as well, including members of Elizabeth's farming family through to a clique of drinking partners in Máire Neeson's bar where they found considerable solace. In this setting, the counter claim was that the Brown family was always involved in some dispute or other at the pier (that is, they were unashamedly lower class); and they had behaved quite irresponsibly in allowing Dervla to turn her back on her parents and take up residence in Mickey's already over-crowded home. Allowing her to stay there exacerbated a difficult situation, and it was also 'asking for trouble', as a woman from the village put it, referring to the widespread assumption that at the pier pregnancy precedes marriage rather than vice versa (yet another lower-class trait).

The third point is that the response to such a sequence of events draws extensively on the current stock of knowledge in the community, and it adds to that stock. This is why getting into sustained dispute with other locally born people can prove hazardous: information which one might be relieved to have had well buried is excavated and disseminated with alacrity. In this instance, Dervla's parents undoubtedly bore the major cost, for whilst it was widely assumed that the objection to Mickey came chiefly from Elizabeth, not only had she married downwards in her own family's eyes, but she now spent a good deal of time in Máire's bar where the routine drinking, smoking and gossiping at all hours of the day earned the bar and its regulars widespread disapproval. In the course of this dispute, a country woman who had been Elizabeth's friend for many years told me that she was increasingly distancing herself from Elizabeth because of the questionable company she now kept. In short, the dispute provoked a great deal of gossip and intense public scrutiny, and the damning conclusion was that Dervla's parents had nothing to be especially proud or stand-offish about.

THE MANAGEMENT OF REPAIR

It is through social situations such as this that Inveresk measures up to its reputation as a tough little place. Individual reputations can be man-handled and family ones hounded down under these circumstances. The extended family loyally rallies round to protect the shared name and the common identity, a near-routine process which residents capture well when they say: 'Kick a McBrearty at one end of the country and a McBrearty at the other end of the pier will scream'. But the effect of such mobilisation is to reinforce the emergent cleavage, to make a costly encounter even more so, not least because knowledge about a significant dispute spills across any domain-specific boundary and gets disseminated throughout the community. All reputations are vulnerable under these circumstances.

DIFFERENCE AND DISPUTE

In the dispute between the Coogans and Browns, it was essentially pier folk who caught wind of early tensions. The Coogan household is situated on the boundary between village and pier, but because of their involvement in fishing, their affiliation was primarily towards the pier. Subsequently, however, both relatives in the country and friends in the village were drawn in as Liam and Elizabeth looked for support. Finally, as well as the fracas in the village ensuring that every immediate and past detail of the dispute circulated throughout its bars, news spread further through Joseph Barry, a part-time fisherman living in the country, who told a considerable number of neighbours, of which I was one, his side of the story.

So one essential point about conflict in Inveresk is that it is exceptionally difficult to compartmentalise and contain: a residence-based dispute between families feeds into rivalry between boats, a conflict over a boundary between cottages gets tied up with rivalry between community associations,[2] and so on. On one notorious occasion, a friendly darts match between teams from the pier's two public bars degenerated into a free-for-all because, as the teams lined up, it became evident that their composition mirrored some especially virulent rivalries between boat crews. By the same token, though, it is precisely the multiplex character of relations within domains which brings many disputes to an early close. Whilst occupational relations between immediate neighbours, for example, might escalate tensions on the one hand, on the other it makes especially difficult their remaining at odds over the long term. This is not to deny that some disputes prove remarkably enduring: but some games are seen to be not worth the candle, the incidents which triggered dispute are acknowledged in retrospect to be insignificant, and more than any other consideration, those in dispute have to face up to the need to re-establish working relations as soon as possible.

This is done by reinstating the ritual minutiae of interpersonal conduct which are an inescapable feature of everyday life but which have been put on hold because of dispute. For example, I indicated at the outset that there are only two routes into Inveresk. One of these carries all vehicular traffic to Foxtown and Westport so that cars from the community are constantly passing one another on this narrow road. Once one has driven past Kilglass, which is the first substantial settlement out of Inveresk, it is no longer necessary to raise one's finger from the driving wheel to an oncoming vehicle driven by a fellow resident; beyond that point, one is outside the community's significant social compass. Before reaching Kilglass, however, this is imperative if one wishes to avoid giving offence, even if one has met and talked with the oncoming driver several times already that day. When people fall out then, the first step they take is to

58   A WORLD OF FINE DIFFERENCE

stop acknowledging one another in this fashion. But when one party decides the time is right to repair the breach, this is done by reinstating the routine of the raised finger.[3]

Especially among housewives going to the village stores each day, similar small rituals can be broken off and then resumed without loss of face.[4] Among men, it is attendance at the bar which most facilitates social repair. On one occasion, Dermot Fitzgibbon and I were driving from the pier via the village to his home on Hill Road after a particularly miserable day's fishing. We were soaked to the bone and very cold, and we had no fish. Yet as we entered the village, he suddenly stopped the van and insisted we both have a drink in Seamus O'Donnell's public house. Joseph Barry had that moment gone into the bar, which at that time of day would assuredly be empty, a good opportunity to paper over rising tensions concerning tangled nets. As soon as the three of us had each downed a pint of stout and a whiskey chaser, all bought by Dermot, he used our bedraggled condition as an excuse to resume the journey home.

The alternative to strategic engagement when conflict threatens is tactical avoidance, and this too is integral to everyday life. Despite its overwhelming informality, many residents have routine patterns of daily behaviour which involve encounters with relatives, visits to the general stores, and regular trips out of the community. Inveresk residents are exceptionally familiar with the routines of others, which allows individuals to avoid encountering those with whom they happen to be on bad terms.[5] The information is essential in order to avoid those encounters in which totally ignoring another resident would be near impossible, in the cramped space of the post office for example.

Residents are especially adept at anticipating others' locations and activities from the presence of a parked car, a bicycle or a child's pram, the company which he or she has been keeping of late, or even how individuals have been recently dressed. On leaving the cottage I was renting from a farmer in 1993, his wife asked where I was heading, to which the reply was another farmer's wife living two kilometres distant. I was unlikely to find her at home, said my inquisitor, because she had seen the other woman at her gate 'dressed to go out'. It was coming up to 11 a.m., so – imagining that I could play this game too – I surmised she might have been on her way to Mass. 'Ah no, not dressed like that she wasn't, not our Mrs Whelan', was the sharp retort. 'Most likely she's gone to do a bit o' shopping in Westport', and so it proved, of course.

Much later that day, I became involved in a drinking session with fishermen at the pier, one of whom persuaded me to peel off to have a drink or two in the village. As we entered this space, we were preceded by Jim Loach, the aggressive part-owner of the other pier bar, who darted

DIFFERENCE AND DISPUTE

into Seamus O'Donnell's establishment. 'We're not going in there while that bastard's around', declared my companion, and so we headed towards the farmers' house until Fergal realised that the van belonging to his sister's husband, whose big boat he had recently quit following a dispute over shares, was parked outside. This brought us to the Night Club, but this was off-limits to Fergal because of some trouble with a couple of Máire Neeson's regular customers the previous weekend. The remaining option was Conor Neeson's bar, but not only did Fergal have a poor opinion of the whole family, he also especially disliked the eldest son (a minor clerk and 'jumped-up little prick' in several fishermen's eyes), who would be serving behind the bar because this was his Friday night routine. So we trudged back to exactly where we had started off at the pier. But at least we were in possession of an up-to-date map of who was drinking where in the village, and this was duly transmitted to whoever expressed an interest.

The significance of certain avoidance strategies is open to interpretation. They can be taken to mean that the resident holds another in such poor regard that any further contact would be unthinkable, or they can be interpreted as attempts to avoid further escalation. For the most part, the latter applies because, as people frequently say, 'you have to live in the place'. They recognise that for most inhabitants there is negligible chance of moving elsewhere: one is always going to encounter residents whom one does not particularly take to; and unlike the situation in large and segregated urban environments, such people can never be avoided altogether. A pragmatic stance is necessary, and this means being as tolerant as one can possibly be. Tolerance is not so much a moral quality as a practical necessity if one's life in Inveresk is going to be relatively straightforward most of the time.

MOORINGS AND MAYHEM

In certain respects, however, this has to be a counsel of perfection: for not only does the community measure up to its wider reputation as a tough little place, but certain developments also seriously compound it. The various stratagems of dispute containment simply prove unequal to the intensity of the conflicts generated between extended families. In order to detail this, I now turn to the second conflict in which the Brown family was involved in 1987 and 1988. I also focus on this particular dispute because, as we shall see, it raises questions about the relation between grassroots circumstances and the wider exercise of power, a consideration which will be addressed at length in chapter 7.

Because of the port's small size and an increase in the number of boats moored there, overcrowding has become a problem. Yet there was no precedent for the hostilities which embroiled Eddie McGreal, 56 and born and bred at the pier, and Larry Elliott, 37, who married into the Brown family in the late 1970s. The McGreal family is every bit as tight-knit as the Browns: both place a premium on family loyalty; and each is connected through marriage and friendship with at least one other extended family, the Browns with the McGarritys, the McGreals with the Sweeneys.

During the mid-1980s, the two men had adjacent moorings in the port, Eddie for his big boat owned since the 1950s, Larry for a punt. The former was not especially active by local standards, the latter (although not a commercial fisherman before marrying into Inveresk) had worked assiduously at different types of coastline fishing until Bord Iascaigh Mhara provided him with the finance to build a new 35 foot boat, the first time this had happened in Inveresk. Since Larry was soon to take delivery of this vessel, he was increasingly concerned that, in his view, Eddie had shifted his moorings closer to those of his punt. This would hinder the movement of his new vessel once in place, so he went to Eddie's pier bungalow to discuss the issue. No sooner had he explained the predicament than Eddie slammed the door in his face. His only comment was that no blow-in had any rights to moorings in Inveresk, certainly none which would take precedence over his own as someone born and bred at the pier.

This response bore out Eddie's local reputation as a curmudgeonly character. So Larry turned to his wife's sister's husband, who was also his close associate, Barry McGarrity. He had occupied the position of harbour constable for the previous 13 years, which meant that he was responsible to the county council for harbour maintenance. He too went to see Eddie who responded that Larry's moorings had moved, not his, and that it was Barry's responsibility to rectify the situation; he had no intention of accommodating an 'uppity blow-in' ('uppity' because he was now about to acquire a new boat). When Barry replied that his judgement supported Larry's claim, the response was fairly predictable: the Elliotts, the Browns and the McGarritys were lining up to run the show at the pier. By this time, naturally, all domain residents had got wind of the rising dispute.

Delivery of the new vessel was drawing close, so Larry took a sterner line. A solicitor from Westport was hired to inform Eddie that unless he adjusted his moorings, further action would result. The response was unexpected: Eddie counter-claimed through his own solicitor that Larry's moorings had prevented, and were still preventing, him from properly pursuing his livelihood. He further indicated that, unless Larry returned his moorings to their previous position, he would be sued for Eddie's lost earnings. Not long afterwards, the new boat arrived to a major celebration by the Brown family and those associated with them. But the boat had to be moored against the harbour wall, and winter weather was approaching.

DIFFERENCE AND DISPUTE 61

The two factions were well organised when the dispute came before the circuit court in Westport. With the McGreal and Sweeney families in attendance, the plaintiff claimed £12,500 in lost earnings, and in his submission Eddie called as a witness Sheila Dawson who handled the accounts in her husband's fish buying enterprise. On the basis of cash payments to comparable boats over the disputed period, she affirmed this was a reasonable estimate of lost income. What was not known to the court, but was legendary throughout Inveresk, was that three years previously, Larry and Johnny Dawson had been business partners in Inveresk. However, they fell out quite spectacularly and neither they nor their wives had exchanged a word since. In the community, this entirely accounted for Sheila's endorsement of Eddie's claim. Also appearing on Eddie's behalf were members of the Sweeney family, Joseph Barry who had long been a close friend of Eddie, and likewise a much older man, Richard Scully, who had been the harbour constable in the 1950s. His presence confirmed that at least some in the prominent Scully family were supporting the McGreal–Sweeney faction.

On the other side, Larry's case was initially advanced with a series of photographs which he had taken over the years to show that his moorings had remained fixed. He was fully supported by Barry McGarrity who appeared in his current role of harbour master. The defendant's other witnesses were John and James Brown, his brothers-in-law, who testified that he had not changed his moorings since being allocated them, and that, in any event, a skipper worthy of the name should have been capable of moving a boat the size of Eddie's vessel out of the moorings currently in place. The circuit court quickly decided in Larry's favour. Eddie was to adjust his moorings, he was not to interfere further with the defendant's boat or fishing livelihood, and his claim for damages was rejected.

For a brief period, it seemed this might be an end to the matter. Instead, there was a mammoth escalation: Eddie decided to appeal to the High Court, an unprecedented step as far as Inveresk was concerned. During the next year or so, several incidents exacerbated relations, until mid-1998 when the rival factions assembled in the distant metropolitan High Court. In this cramped setting it was impossible for the two sides to ignore or evade one another: everyone was acutely uncomfortable. The appearance of new supporters in both camps provoked a lot of speculation. Eddie was now accompanied by Tod Cashman, a young fisherman from yet another prominent pier family: 'What the fuck is Cashman doing in with that lot? Is he a cousin of the McGreals, or what? So what's he going to fucking well say in there?' was the response of James Brown. My appearance in the company of the Elliott and Brown families, with whom I had a long association, sparked a similar reaction. Speculation spread

62 A WORLD OF FINE DIFFERENCE

that I intended to draw on my research findings on the local fishing industry which extended as far back as 1983.

At that moment, it was of greater concern to Larry and Carmel Elliott that the Queen's Counsel engaged at inordinate expense had no experience of boats or fishing whatsoever. Even in late briefing sessions, the most elementary details had to be explained several times over, to the great concern of the Elliotts and their supporters. Finally, extreme uncertainty and insecurity on both sides was compounded by delay. For four days in succession, a procession of vehicles set off from Inveresk early in the morning, only to return at night without the case having been called. On the fourth day, all were told that it was to be delayed a further six months, a prospect as daunting to those supporting Larry Elliott as it was to those backing Eddie McGreal, not least because relations at the pier were at an all time low.

THE SIGNIFICANCE AND THE CONSEQUENCES OF PUBLIC DISPUTE

There are several points to establish about the way this dispute unfolded. The first is that previously the relationship between the Elliotts and Browns, and the McGreals, was uncomplicated by pier standards. It had none of the multiplex qualities which, I argued earlier, can serve to contain the range and the intensity of dispute. Despite both the Browns and the McGreals being long-established pier families, there was strikingly little by way of historical connection between them. Specifically, Larry and Eddie had had little to do with one another over the years: there were no kin, work or friendship ties which might have held in check the escalation of dispute between them.

Secondly, this took on importance when the distinction between born and bred and blow-in residents was invoked by Eddie to justify his uncompromising position. Especially at the pier where, over the past two decades, several men from beyond Inveresk have brought boats to the harbour, the distinction between outsiders and insiders is of undoubted significance to some, but by no means all; indeed, how consequential it might be is a recurrent topic in domain discourse. Eddie was certainly not alone in the judgement that a blow-in had no rights there by comparison with someone like himself: he was simply unusual in expressing his views so openly, and then repeating them as the dispute escalated. Without doubt, his position drew some support from other pier men resentful of Larry's acquisition of a new boat, which was custom-built with state finance. Most have to be content with vessels which have had several owners.

DIFFERENCE AND DISPUTE 63

Nevertheless at no stage, thirdly, was it suggested that Larry's blow-in status might compromise the response from his affines. By this time, he had been married for almost 15 years and Carmel was a dominant influence on all interrelations within this large family network, as well as its linkage to the McGarritys. Although the couple lived in an old cottage away from the pier, a substantial part of every day was spent in the family home or in the port. By virtue of owning a big boat, Larry was able to take on his brothers-in-law as sharemen. So the Brown and McGarrity families rallied round Larry from the outset, as was the case with the McGreal–Sweeney faction in which Maeve McGreal, who had married in from the Sweeneys, played an integrative role similar to that of Carmel Elliott.

As a result of these factors, the important consequence for present purposes is that as the conflict between the two factions escalated, it was monitored across the entire social landscape of Inveresk: in no sense could its political impact or knowledge about it be restricted to the pier. The more the dispute developed momentum, the more it attracted attention from residents in all three domains of Inveresk – and considerably further afield, including neighbouring communities. It has to be remembered that this dispute unfolded at much the same time that the Browns and the Coogans were at public loggerheads. The combined effect, therefore, was to reinforce and compound the pronounced qualities of the pier as a distinct domain in Inveresk as a whole. Close cooperation on the one hand, outright conflict on the other, were the defining properties of pier life now crystallised in the same sequence of unfolding events.

The identity of the pier as a qualitatively different place to that of the village and the country was not just confirmed but also substantially augmented. Its reputation as a place where 'things happen that couldn't happen anywhere else' was not just borne out but amplified further. All this did much to confirm the cultural distinctiveness of the pier domain, and thus by necessary implication the particular identities of the village and the country as places which, in comparative terms, exhibited different qualities again. Earlier it was argued that when developments in one domain confirm its distinctiveness as a particular place, its juxtaposition with the other two inevitably ensures that further comparisons are made. This unfolding series of events proved a striking case in point. Whenever I discussed the meaning of these developments with country residents, I was told time and again that, whilst such conflicts were much as to be expected from pier folk, it was inconceivable that anything similar could materialise in the country. Farmers and their wives in particular were aghast at the mayhem which they saw to be breaking out at the other end of the community. It confirmed for them the value of the farm family keeping

64 A WORLD OF FINE DIFFERENCE

itself to itself, of keeping neighbours at modest arm's length, of behaving in restrained fashion, and so on. To this extent, the conflicts of this period confirmed not only the social distinctiveness of the pier but also the integrity of its cultural boundary vis-à-vis Inveresk's other two domains.

THE MORALITY OF DISPUTE

In conclusion, however, it is important to acknowledge that in the final stages of this all-important dispute, there emerged another, distinctly contrasting local response to those drawn out thus far. By this stage it will be clear that this was not only a protracted dispute but also an expensive one. Even before the fatal step into the High Court, both sides had to bear the cost of legal fees for roughly two years, and on each occasion when they had to brief solicitors, prepare their respective cases and appear in court, they had to cancel a day or more of fishing. When the action in the High Court eventuated, the costs faced by both parties soared since Queen's Counsels had to be engaged and more working hours had to be set aside for preparation of their cases.

The striking new development at this later stage was that the supporters of the two protagonists began to question openly and strongly the conflict being taken to this extreme. From within their own supporters' ranks, the view was increasingly expressed that both Eddie and Larry were in an untenable situation from which no one could emerge with any degree of success or satisfaction – certainly, nobody from Inveresk. As the combatants assembled in the High Court in late 1988 for what would prove to be the last time, Barry McGarrity surveyed the scene as Larry's faction members waited yet again for the case to be called: 'What a total waste of fucking time this is, now. 'Tis alright for these solicitor fellars, dashing up and down in fancy wigs and gowns, and all. Their wages is coming in whatever they do. But ours is just running out, just running right out.' He concluded: ''Tis a bloody disgrace. They're just wasting our time as if it's no fucking consequence at all.'

Shortly after this outburst, Larry himself rejoined the group in an anxious state following a lengthy session with his legal counsel: 'I don't like this, not a bit of it. We could be in there [that is, in the court] any minute now and this fellar still hasn't got a fucking clue as to what we're on about. He's not an idea as to what it's like at the pier, he hasn't a fucking clue as to what boats and moorings are all about.' John Brown, the brother-in-law to whom Larry was closest, took all this in: 'And he's supposed to be on our side! So you can be fucking sure it'll be the same with the judge. None of this lot have ever been on a boat, never mind our pier.' Then he added: 'Larry boy, this woman [the judge] won't understand

DIFFERENCE AND DISPUTE 65

a word of what you, all of us, will put in front of her, not a fucking word.' Larry acknowledged this with 'We're in the hands of the gods here and that's a fucking fact', at which point the solicitor reappeared to warn that when the group finally entered the court they should spread themselves around its benches: 'The judges here don't like to see you sitting like a clan, or a tribe, or something like that. So spread yourselves all over the place.' The instruction could scarcely have been bettered in underscoring the gulf which existed between the ordinary folk from the rural periphery and the powerful from the centre who were about to sit in judgement on them. What the former considered important – sitting solidly together in an uncomplicated expression of family loyalty – was what the latter considered wholly unacceptable.

The sentiment which was now palpable and growing on both sides, then, was that the two fishermen were locked into a destructive, alienating process from which there could be no final advantage. Equally important by this stage, similar sentiments were being voiced in the community at large that the conflict between the two fishermen and their supporters had spiralled out of control. It had escalated to the point at which the leading protagonists faced financial ruin with deleterious consequences for many others. For this they were to be equally condemned. In the summary judgement of a village publican to his regular drinkers: 'They're a pair o' prideful fucking eejits whose quarrel's brought nothing but trouble for everybody.' The litany of objections was considerable: the pier was divided, people had stopped talking to one another, conversations in bars became overheated, and all this made the community look bad in the eyes of those in neighbouring communities. Worst of all, the only beneficiaries would be members of the powerful legal profession. Lawyers, solicitors, Queen's Counsels and the rest would benefit, but the two protagonists might well be in debt to the point at which one or the other, perhaps even both, would have to sell off the productive assets they had gone into court to protect.

What was ultimately striking, then, about this final stage was that, whilst the course of events had assuredly compounded several lines of difference and division within Inveresk, the community as a whole now arrived at a collective moral judgement which strongly sanctioned the two combatants. Unrestrained pride on their part, coupled with uncritical loyalty from their supporters, had produced a practically and morally untenable situation from which only powerful outsiders could gain. The local population might lose scarce resources which it could ill afford to surrender: their customary state of powerlessness in relation to the outside world was being played out yet again.

This generalised feeling of powerlessness amongst Inveresk folk will be returned to in a later chapter. Suffice it to say here that resentment about it surfaces regularly in this peripheral community, and it is the source of frustration and anger too. At this stage the important issue is that the rivalry between the two fishermen had culminated in a situation from which the community as a whole looked to be the likely loser. It was this prospect to which residents generally took exception, and they made their judgement known. So whilst at one level differences and divisions within Inveresk had been compounded, at another an idiom of shared community interests was being articulated, along with the moral injunction that every individual should be as cognisant of collective, communal interests as well as his or her own specific ones. It is the details of this undercurrent of a common morality, so often hidden by the proliferation of difference and division, which will be looked at more closely in the next chapter.

5

THE GENEROSITY
OF COMMUNITY

In early 1993, I talked at some length about the recent politics of regional farming with Leo White, an older farmer and prominent member of the Irish Farmers' Association who resides in Dromore, the community directly across the bay from Inveresk. This farmer is well familiar with Inveresk. He has lived within walking distance of it all his life: he is first cousin to Roland Dowd who is amongst the most successful farmers in the townland; indeed, the two men are close friends and their annual holidays involve travelling together to agricultural shows. Yet when we had finished talking about farm politics, Leo told me that, on the whole, he had little time for Inveresk folk because he found them clannish and ungenerous. We have already encountered the accusation that Inveresk people are obsessed with their insular world. But Leo went on to say he found them ungenerous in the sense that they judged not only outsiders but also themselves too harshly. He put it this way: 'To live comfortable-like in small places like ours, you have to be generous in dealings with one another. But *they're not*, not at all, Inveresk people have *never* been blessed with a generosity of spirit.'

Within Inveresk, the reality on this count at least appears different: for in a manner which contrasts sharply with the pattern of differentiation, division and dispute concentrated upon thus far, it is possible for Inveresk residents to extend a supporting hand to one another, to display exceptional generosity in fact, and in the course of doing so to express their attachment to the community as a whole. Practically and symbolically, they express a substantial commitment to Inveresk as a social and political entity which encompasses and supersedes the lines of difference that are such an integral part of everyday life. In the course of doing so, they build on the sense of shared moral obligation to the community at large that finally surfaced in the disastrous conflict between Larry Elliot and Eddie McGreal.

68   A WORLD OF FINE DIFFERENCE

In this chapter and the next, my concern is to detail this contrasting dimension of Inveresk experience because this is the community's consistently paradoxical quality. How is a sense of collective unity and integrity constituted between the pier, village and country domains? What are the resources that make possible this broader attachment to Inveresk as an encompassing place? How is this more expansive sense of place translated into appropriately meaningful symbolic activities? Far from this being a form of mechanical solidarity as a Durkheimian sociologist might view it, the argument developed here is that this broader sense of emplacement has to be strategically pulled off by the residents. Just as the generation of dispute is politically accomplished by variously motivated agents, so too with public expressions of Inveresk as a broader, integrated place with its own distinctive character.

FROM THE DISCOURSE OF DOMAIN
TO THE DISCOURSE OF COMMUNITY

In chapter 3 it was argued that such was the detail and the intensity with which people converse about their place-specific affairs, that it was heuristically appropriate to label routine day-to-day talk as domain discourse. Yet it will be evident from the conclusion to the preceding chapter that this is only part of the picture. Inveresk folk are also in command of a broader discourse which transcends domain boundaries and interests, and this was evident when residents from throughout the community reflected on the wider impact of the dispute between the two fishermen and their supporters. It is this broader discourse that is integral to the mounting of activities and happenings in which the spirit of communal generosity and well-being is embedded. Like all social boundaries, those between Inveresk's domains are distinctly permeable, and this being so, information about significant issues becomes the common conversational currency of committed members in the community at large.

There are a number of factors which contribute to this, but three warrant emphasis. The first comprises the many linkages of a primarily economic nature which exist between those in different domains. Notwithstanding the predominance of one means of livelihood in each domain and the absence of significant linkages between them, there is an extensive web of cross-cutting economic ties in which many are involved. Country families use not only the shops in the village but also its garage and the haulage company which provides some the country's bulk transport requirements. In addition to buying from the boats, the village-based fish buyers buy periwinkles from pickers (either housewives or unemployed men) living in all three domains. Each domain has resident

THE GENEROSITY OF COMMUNITY 69

within it self-employed men who do jobs throughout the community: carpenters, builders, painters, as well as odd-job men. Several women drawn from all domains work as hairdressers and seamstresses, whilst others clean private residences, shops and public houses. Some women put together a full-time work schedule from different parcels of part-time work. Ursula McGarrity, for example, is renowned for the hours she works as a waitress in a hotel, a packer in a nearby farm nursery, a house cleaner, and a periwinkle picker, which means that she may traverse all three domains within the course of a working week, and travel outside the community as well.

These ways of making a living serve as critical conduits of information between domains: these residents spread not only their labour but also a great deal of up-to-date information around the community. Likewise significant, as a result of these linkages when one resident changes her or his economic contribution to the community it has ramifications for others, and the situation gets extensively talked about. Miriam Farrelly, for example, is recognised as the community's leading businesswoman because when she returned with her husband and family from a 13-year stay in England, she successfully developed a pier bar which she acquired in run-down condition. A country woman by origin (two of her older unmarried brothers run the family farm, the third lives in the United States), she then established a profitable bed and breakfast enterprise which accommodated anglers who were taken out fishing by her cousin, also a country man. Next, she rented a small building in the village in order to sell knitting wool to residents and visitors. This provided work for local painters and carpenters, as did the renovation of rooms below the shop when Miriam decided to sell afternoon teas. (To furnish this, she acquired tables, chairs and other items from Rose Morrissey who owned a village shop and wanted extra space to set up post office facilities.) In the summer, Miriam's new enterprise proved so successful that she took on two young women to help expand the bed and breakfast business. They were both from farm families and therefore in Miriam's eyes entirely reliable. Also they would return to school as the tourist season ended, so it would not be necessary to lay them off, a step any Inveresk entrepreneur finds difficult to take when local people are involved.

Inside Inveresk, these are by no means humdrum concerns. This kind of economic connectedness means that everything is common knowledge about such enterprises and the individuals who run them, in Miriam's case cutting directly across the boundaries between pier, village and country. The second factor which compounds these inter-domain linkages are exceptions to the work and residence patterns detailed in chapter 2. Not all fishermen are resident at the pier, nor are all entrepreneurs concentrated

70 A WORLD OF FINE DIFFERENCE

in the village. Two leading fishermen (both with teenage sons who fish) own older houses in the village; boats used to be launched there from a sheltered slipway. Four fishermen live in the country either in old cottages which they have rebuilt over the years, or in modern bungalows constructed by a local builder. These men live in the country at least in part because they and their wives have found pier life too dispute-ridden and demanding. Dermot Fitzgibbon and his family live in a country bungalow in order to put some distance between his work at the pier and family life, although they are unusual in more ways than one: they entered Inveresk as a family unit, they had no property in the place, nor a network of relations to ease their passage into community life.

Such exceptions are important because information about events ongoing in one domain gets disseminated elsewhere via the distinctive social networks they have built up. One of Dermot's friends, for example, is a farmer, whilst his wife's acquaintances are drawn from the country (a farmer's wife), the village (a schoolteacher) and the pier (an ex-schoolteacher married to a businessman). The third influence on the movement of information cross-domain is the considerable number of wage-earners and unemployed people who are scattered throughout Inveresk. Because of their occupational status, they are considerably less attached than most to any particular location. Wage-earning in general is not highly regarded, even wage-earners themselves will say: 'It's just a job, there can be no satisfaction in working for somebody else'. In social terms, these men and women are relatively free from the pressures to which others are subject. Often drawing on a wider circle of friendships than most, they can be relatively indifferent to the distinctions of place so consequential to others.

These considerations are collectively significant. By variously facilitating the transmission of information about residents, events, and associations across the face of Inveresk, they make a distinctive contribution to an ongoing discourse about the community in its entirety. This overarching discourse is, moreover, distilled and condensed, as well as built upon and elaborated, in particular sites as well. I have already described the village as the hub of social traffic for Inveresk. Within it, the village bar owned by Seamus O'Donnell has to be singled out, since it draws together the most heterogeneous clientele. Seamus is heavily involved in regional business organisations and in party politics, so that his personal network beyond Inveresk is sometimes useful to others. Inside the community (unlike his brother with the farmers' house), he is aligned with neither pier nor country folk. The result of these varied factors is that it is not only Seamus's regular customers who are drawn from all domains, but also the more substantial, uncommitted clientele which moves between public houses on a regular basis. This means that the

THE GENEROSITY OF COMMUNITY

information circulating through his bar is considerably more diverse than anywhere else.

Another site of significance is the household kitchen where the different strands of talk from across the community are woven together. Generally speaking, men and women occupy different niches throughout the working day (only in public houses do spouses work directly alongside one another). The information variously drawn from these is exchanged over the evening meal. But it is also in this context that another major source of cross-domain talk gets disseminated: this is the input provided by teenage children who have the unique status of being drawn together from throughout Inveresk and concentrated in a single site each day, namely the school bus which departs each morning from the centre of the village and arrives in Westport an hour later.

The age-range is 12 to 18, the genders are mixed together as is domain representation, so that the possibility of information pooling is pronounced. In terms of content, what interests older teenagers is often not all that different from what concerns their parents, but the information is exchanged with less discretion. One evening, for example, Dermot Fitzgibbon and I had a few drinks in Seamus O'Donnell's bar after a day spent de-fouling his boat beached on the pier strand. During the nine hours spent on this task, no less than 11 other fishermen had stopped to talk, and one of the casual topics had been extra-marital relations at the pier. One of the fish buyers was rumoured to be having an affair with the wife of the young man he employed as a driver, whilst the buyer's wife had resumed her relationship with a young skipper who was at odds with her husband over outstanding debts. The topic surfaced again in O'Donnell's bar to much ribald commentary. When we arrived at Dermot's country bungalow well into the night, he asked his wife if she knew any details, but it was their 16-year-old son who answered in the affirmative. The whole business had been joked about on the school bus over a week previously, along with a third and more intriguing dalliance of which neither parent was aware.

The example is trivial, but it neatly illustrates how topical information first mooted at the pier was transported into the village and finally carried to the country within the space of a few hours. It underscores that the constituent elements of a community-wide discourse are constantly being created and consolidated, elaborated and refined, over and above the specifics of (in this instance) a technical pier discourse focused on de-fouling a boat. It also leads into the main argument which is that it is in the constitution of the former that coherent narratives about resident individuals and families become the source for determining to what extent they are worthy of community-wide support.

72   A WORLD OF FINE DIFFERENCE

GOSSIP AND NARRATIVE

Evidently gossip is an integral part of social life in this small community. Interpersonal disputes, individual failings, family conflicts, domain hostilities, associational problems, all these and much else are the staple of gossip in Inveresk. It ranges from being moderately amusing about personal foibles through to being quite scandalous where sexual relations are concerned. Residents often say the community is on a par with Peyton Place because of the supposed proliferation of sexual dalliances: it is considered the equal of the Village of Squinting Windows because one's every move is observed, adjudicated, and reported on from behind lace curtains. Gossip is pursued with alacrity and intensity to the extent that, as Berger says of his French village, the community produces 'a living portrait of itself . . . work on it never stops' (1985: 9).

Precisely because it is continuous though, it is appropriate in this context to distinguish between gossip and narrative, the latter being a cumulative product of the former and a resource on the basis of which serious moral judgements can be made within Inveresk. This is by no means to suggest that gossip per se is not a serious matter. But however much anthropologists attempt to redefine gossip, it remains in interactional terms a brief and intensive encounter between two or three individuals in which information is transmitted about an absent other whose reputation is in varying degree maligned.[1] In broader terms, however, the important issue is that any gossip encounter draws on an extensive stock of knowledge about all the actors involved, and it significantly adds to that stock as well. Above all, it becomes incorporated into ever-evolving narratives about the community and those who populate it.[2] It is in the content of these often comprehensive narratives that residents find the details they require to make decisions at times of personal, familial and indeed communal crisis.[3]

There are several important points to establish about these narratives, the first being that they are the product of multiple voices and the outcome of many judgements spread over lengthy periods. A narrative does not have a clear beginning (or a definite ending, for that matter) because it draws on accretions of knowledge from way back. It may be possible to date an event which becomes the basis for a narrative of consequence: but at least in Inveresk, the biographical details of prominent participants are frequently mined from some time back in order to make sense of a happening's complexity. So when a narrative begins is always an arbitrary judgement.

The second property is that its meaning is highly variable. Whilst there may be broad agreement over its essential contours – the major participants, the distinct stages, the resources at stake – its significance to those

THE GENEROSITY OF COMMUNITY 73

inspecting it close up, will inevitably vary a good deal. Thus, to glance backwards for a moment, the narrative to emerge out of the dispute between Larry Elliott and Eddy McGreal was especially subject to multiple interpretations, and none of them could be readily privileged over others. How the dispute started, what the motives behind it were, why some and not others were drawn into the dispute, were all issues subject to variable interpretation as it became incorporated into the stock of significant community storylines.

Third, and here especially important, notwithstanding the acknowledgement of arbitrary interpretation which unites the first and second considerations, a sense of belonging to the community at large is embedded precisely in the understanding and appreciation of these narratives. Whilst the particularities of interpretation and the details of comprehension will always be open to wide-ranging dispute, what is ultimately important is that the ability to act as an interpreter of, and the capacity to function as a contributor to, the significant narratives in circulation over time, constitute key criteria of community membership in their own right. Interpretation and belonging are one and the same local experience in this view, so that by way of a corollary argument, the boundary to Inveresk as a community is to be drawn where residents' ability both to interpret and to contribute to its more important narratives markedly diminishes.[4]

The intricacy and the complexity of these narratives are especially striking qualities. In addition to main characters, they incorporate subsidiary players: as well as the dominant narrative, prior and ongoing minor storylines are underway; and because the events they relate are protracted, it has to be established as to what extent the present can be understood in its own terms, or as a product of the past, in order to allocate responsibility. In short, any reasonable comprehension of these narratives has to be prefaced by sustained engagement with the community. What is of most consequence is the wealth of prior local experience required in order to comment openly on such narratives as they unfold, that is to contribute in (often gossipy) talk to their elaboration in the specific, situational settings of Inveresk itself. The requirement here is not only knowing *what* to say, but also precisely *how* to say it, and exactly *who* to say it to. It is a question of knowing more-or-less intuitively (which means that everything connected with this has to be very thoroughly learned indeed) what the appropriate speech act is under particular circumstances. All this detail is over and above having understood the implicit refinements of the major narrative in the first instance.[5]

It follows that amongst the population as a whole the level of appreciation of narratives, as well as the capacity to contribute, is highly

74   A WORLD OF FINE DIFFERENCE

variable. This most especially applies to blow-ins who have not been able to acquire this expertise from childhood but have had to do so either on marrying into the community or on entering Inveresk without prior connections. It has already been indicated that incoming spouses often find incorporation difficult. Families who move in as a unit evidently face more substantial obstacles; their initial period is often acutely uncomfortable. They lack the elementary cognitive map which is required to interpret, along with everyone else, the meaning of incidents and the significance of happenings going on around them. Nor do they yet have friendships with locally born residents who might provide them with its preliminary coordinates. Even if they access conversational encounters between locals, in a shop or bar for instance, the meaning of the gossip they hear escapes them; the distance between themselves and those who are established in the place is reinforced.

In short, the narrative is a pivotal resource inasmuch as it has distilled within it information about individuals and families, events and happenings of concern to the community as a whole. It is also a constantly changing crystallisation of current knowledge, reflecting the pace of transformation in Inveresk itself. This being so, when the community is faced with major decisions, its members draw extensively on currently circulating narratives in order to arrive at initiatives they consider well warranted. There are few more important decisions than those concerning residents who are in personal crisis and seem unable to look after themselves, and it is in relation to these that the character of Inveresk as a moral community becomes evident.

COMMUNITY NARRATIVE AND COMMUNAL GENEROSITY

In total (but the figure is necessarily arbitrary) there are about a dozen men and women in Inveresk who are considered especially vulnerable and in need of communal support by virtue of diminished mental faculties or alcohol dependence. Whether these people would be considered officially certifiable by a state institution is irrelevant. It is instead important that the community regards them as vulnerable and that they are mainly considered 'our people'. If at all possible, it is imperative to prevent state agencies moving in on them.

Of critical importance to the narratives about them is that biographical details are well known. Their family backgrounds, the past and present circumstances of their parents and their siblings, the fluctuating fortunes of their own careers, the particular happenings which have made them what they are today, all these are combined in the accounts which circulate,

THE GENEROSITY OF COMMUNITY 75

albeit with discretion and concern that details should not fall into the wrong hands. If they were not born into the community, the narratives centred on them are specific about how they have become permanent residents, and the contribution they have made. These are signal aspects of becoming 'one of us', and so entitled to community support.

As always, a good deal hinges on whether the individual is judged to 'have lived in the place', that is expressed a clear commitment to it in different ways and not just taken up mere residence. There is a clear understanding that, however woeful the individual's circumstances might be, entitlement to the community's support nevertheless has to be earned. When Mrs Klemperer died in early 1993 and was buried at Dromore, neither at the graveside nor the memorial service were more than half-a-dozen mourners present. She had lived in Inveresk for two decades, was well travelled, and had idiosyncratic qualities which usually appeal to Inveresk people. Yet she had lived a life apart (substantially indexed by the fact that she was always *Mrs* Klemperer), hence the relative lack of interest in her passing on.

This is not to say that, subsequent to reviewing narrative details, rendering assistance to others is a straightforward business. It is complicated for a start by unswerving recognition that those who require support are nevertheless individuals whose sensibilities warrant due respect. In the case of three older men who are alcohol dependent, for example, each now lives alone, is no longer economically active, suffers from a variety of illnesses, and spends the greater part of the pension on beer and spirits. From time to time, each man has also been institutionalised for remedial treatment, but to no lasting effect. Yet no one suggests that they should be removed from the community: it is in Inveresk alone that they can be looked after in such a way that they can retain their dignity. Donal Donaghue, for example, is regularly fed in the farmers' house by Peadar and Nuala O'Donnell, but there is no contradiction between them doing this and serving him alcohol. To continue to drink is his choice, and that choice has to be respected, not least since he has always been a fully fledged, highly individualistic, member of the community.

In instances like this – and there are a good number of them in Inveresk – it is particular networks which care for the person at hazard. But this is activity held to epitomise community spirit, especially the sense of moral responsibility which is considered the acme of community membership.[6] Apparently free from self-interest or material considerations, these altruistic efforts comprise the other, positive face of Inveresk, not divided and disputatious, but generous and gratuitous, and therefore subject to laudatory comments from most quarters. Naturally, some degree of kudos attaches to individuals who provide extensive assistance

76 A WORLD OF FINE DIFFERENCE

to others, but that is about the limit of the gains that flow, for those who are down-and-out have little of material consequence to offer. What is gained is community recognition and little else, but in a place like Inveresk where residents can more than match up to their reputation for treating one another harshly, this is by no means inconsequential.

There are also critical occasions on which the community as a broader entity rallies in support of those in difficulty, a more complicated process than those involving circumscribed social networks. In such instances, the importance of narratives about particular individuals and those around them becomes transparent: they become the basis for the community at large making a moral assessment of the worth of those involved, and thus determining what assistance is to be given. Needless to say, this kind of circumstance eventuates irregularly, but inasmuch as there is a sizeable minority of people in Inveresk who are on the subsistence borderline, aged, out of regular employment, suffering from major illness, and so on, rarely does a year pass by without the community being faced with a crisis of some moment. It is on such occasions that the moral value which residents attach to the community as a whole not only comes to the fore but is also tested, sometimes to the limit.

LOOKING AFTER CATHLEEN

One such sequence of events was set in motion when a small, hastily written poster appeared in the window of the general store in the village. It announced 'An Emergency Meeting' at 9.00 that evening in the community centre. Across the bottom of the sheet was scrawled 'Re: The Recent Fire Tragedy'. The announcement was unsigned but the priest's handwriting was well known, and its cryptic message reflected the assumption that the whole community already knew what was afoot. The previous night, a mobile home belonging to Cathleen Barry had been destroyed by fire, along with all her possessions and those of her two small children. The mobile home was on a rough patch of ground at the pier. As he surveyed the scene, the priest announced he would organise some assistance for Cathleen, and the public meeting was to be the first step.

The first insight came even before the meeting began. Six older women arrived by car from Dromore for the weekly bingo session in the community hall. This had been cancelled to make way for the meeting, but no one had thought to inform them. Although they all knew Cathleen well, it was not suggested they attend the meeting, and so they left in somewhat bad humour. From the outset, this was emphatically and unambiguously defined as Inveresk business.

THE GENEROSITY OF COMMUNITY 77

When the meeting began, some 43 residents were present: 33 were women; 18 were from the pier, 14 from the village and the remainder were country folk. All were aware of Cathleen's chequered career, albeit unevenly since the narrative focused on the Barry family was marked by considerable sensitivity.[7] The family home was a two-storey dwelling situated in the country where Cathleen's father, long deceased, had been a farm labourer and jolter.[8] This was currently occupied by Cathleen's aged mother, her brother Joseph, and her sister Eithne; another sister lived in the family home from time to time. This was an especially strained family because some of its members were afflicted by mental illness, and Joseph repeatedly fought with his elder brother, who lived in an adjacent bungalow, over rights to the family property. The younger brother, his wife, and their children lived in another mobile home on the outskirts of the village, and for them too life was difficult.

Conflict over Cathleen's marriage had added immeasurably to this knotty set of circumstances. Just nine years previously, she had married a labourer from Foxtown. His employment was insecure, his behaviour unpredictable, and in his small family home relations between Cathleen and her mother-in-law became strained, especially following the birth of their second child. Leaving her husband behind, Cathleen returned to her place of birth where she maintained an uncertain day-to-day existence. Then, unknown to her brothers who were at least united in opposition to him, she resumed occasional contact with her husband. Once this was discovered, and following further complications, the ructions were such that she had to move between several rented dwellings before she settled on the cheap mobile home at the pier. Here she joined a close network of pier women, and they were well represented as the meeting got under way.

The priest opened by saying:

> Everyone already knows what happened in this unfortunate circumstance. We should get ourselves together to help out in this. So many people are here that we know we have the full support of the community in all this. Cathleen's caravan is totally bunched, but thanks be to God the family wasn't hurt at all.

He explained that he had arranged two weeks' accommodation for the family in the village, so that everyone knew the situation had to be dealt with swiftly. Cathleen, who was not present, would welcome any help from the community: 'Everything is in your hands. From now on the decisions are your own. But a committee is a real necessity.'

Meetings in Inveresk always stall at this point until the priest stands up once again and calls for nominations for a chairman. True to form, one of his staunch supporters nominated the priest himself. This was followed

78 A WORLD OF FINE DIFFERENCE

by a village-based male wage-earner becoming treasurer, a farmer's wife being elected secretary, and two women from the pier (both Cathleen's close friends) making up the committee. The priest commented: 'Well, that's real progress, all right. We've got a representative group here already. So where do people think we should go next? I'm told we need about £2000 to replace the old home.'

A number of proposals were made. A woman from the pier proposed a door-to-door collection; a pier youth offered all entrance takings from the Friday dance which he organised; the recent Christmas concert could be repeated; the proceedings from bingo sessions would be donated. In all, six firm proposals were made with, in each case, one person to preside, whereupon the priest interjected: 'Now we're really getting somewhere. The committee can take over here and we'll settle the details.' The clear message was that most present should leave at this point, but no one moved. Evidently all felt they had more to contribute, and the priest resigned himself to this with a shrug of the shoulders.

Once it had been agreed that £2000 would be the target, a fortnight-long schedule was drawn up to accommodate all the proposals. The only one to provoke dispute was the door-to-door collection, and it was triggered by a farmer's wife, who wondered aloud if this was entirely appropriate: 'Cathleen's family might not like it because, y'know, it looks a lot like a charity collection, going from door to door like that'. Immediately, Cathleen's pier friend on the committee rejoindered that Cathleen herself would have no objection: '. . . and anyway', she added pointedly, 'this isn't any of the family's business, you can all see that for yourselves'. This referred to the fact that no member of the extended Barry family was present. Although the comment created momentary embarrassment, it struck home. Then another woman from the pier proposed that only £10 and £20 notes should be accepted because 'this is a big thing, getting a new caravan's a big affair, so everyone should expect to dig deep for it'. After some debate led by the same country woman who had queried the appropriateness of a collection, this proposal was lost on the grounds that older people on a pension would be excluded from contributing. Finally, the sole, but effectively retired, farmer present proposed geographical limits to the collection which would have excluded any household from beyond the townland boundary. The priest spoke firmly against this: neighbouring Dromore, which was also part of his parish, should be included because Cathleen herself had friends there: 'I don't want to see distinctions like that made when an important business like this is on the table'.

Over the next fortnight, two men who regularly travelled outside the community to their respective workplaces set about finding an appropriate,

THE GENEROSITY OF COMMUNITY

second-hand mobile home, the priest arranged a bank account in Cathleen's name, and those individuals who had undertaken to mount particular fund-raising activities went ahead. Meanwhile, in the community at large, the narrative centred on Cathleen and her family was endlessly articulated and interrogated. Most residents in Inveresk were aware that her personal circumstances had, in recent years, become complicated. If they were not, it was not difficult to quickly become well-informed. The problems with her marriage, the disputes between her brothers, her efforts to raise the children whilst separated from her husband, and so on, were all thoroughly reviewed. On top of this, there were many hitherto personal matters concerning the family which became common knowledge. From all these details, the picture to emerge was of a young woman in dire straits, especially since her marriage seemed to be over and she had been effectively put to one side by her siblings.

On the other hand, there emerged a number of qualifying arguments to this ongoing, public discourse. One was whether the community should shoulder the entire responsibility, or whether some of the load should be passed on to the Barry family. The priest had assumed the former, but an increasing number of residents queried this as they took stock of how the family was faring. The eldest brother was fishing successfully at this point of time, and he was drinking heavily in one of the pier bars every night. Some of this money could go to his sister's cause. Another concern was whether Cathleen's personal behaviour really warranted such extensive community support. Despite receiving welfare payments, she seemed to enjoy a fairly full social life in that she was regularly in Máire Neeson's bar. Cathleen might appreciate the new caravan more if she contributed some proportion of the total outlay. And her husband should contribute since the children he had fathered would be the beneficiaries.

It remained incontestable, however, that Cathleen was 'one of us' and 'our responsibility', even though important qualifications were now in circulation. As a country woman on the committee put it over her kitchen table:

> When you look at it altogether, I mean, I know she drinks and she smokes, and perhaps her attitude to life isn't all that it should be, her going into Neeson's and all that, but we've got to get her back on her feet, otherwise she'll be a burden forever, and we've got to keep thinking about the children. I mean, what kind of life are they going to have? Should any little child have to suffer like they're suffering now?

Three weeks on from the first meeting, £2200 had been raised, and a final meeting was called to bring the exercise to a close. Eighteen people were present on this occasion: 14 were women, ten were from the pier, four from the village, and four from the country. It seemed a mere formality, until the priest said that £80 remained uncommitted and asked how it was to be used.

The priest himself proposed that since the mobile home was on a rough piece of land, a low wall might be built around it. Immediately, a male resident from the village objected: 'People aren't expecting us to do that, to go that far with the money they gave us. There'll be a lot of cribbing if we get into that.' The housewife from the country on the committee added by way of support: 'Perhaps it's time, y'know, to let Cathleen look after herself and use the money for some other purpose'. But scarcely had she said this than a pier woman dismissed this as 'mean minded . . . This isn't the time to get bothered about small amounts, the wall should go ahead, so.' When it was suggested that the site owner should be consulted – which everyone knew to be the patriarch of the entrepreneurial Scully family, but he was not mentioned by name – the same woman from the pier replied in dismissive tone that, since neither he nor any member of his family had contributed anything to Cathleen's cause, he was unlikely to become concerned at this stage.

Discussion stalled at this point until the housewife from the country, whose family had long been associated with the Barrys, said: 'Well, Joe has some experience in this. I don't see what's to stop us asking Joe to build a small wall.' This was clearly thought to be a reasonable suggestion, but the priest's response was 'Joe who? Which Joe is it that you're speaking of now?' It had to be pointed out to him that the subject was Joseph Barry, Cathleen's brother. Then quite suddenly the matter was settled by an intervention from Cathleen's closest pier acquaintance: 'Well, if you're asking me, Joseph *should* do it, he should. It's *their* turn now to contribute to helping Cathleen out. It's only right *they* should make a contribution, and at the pier there's a lot of people feeling like that about it.' By 'them' she was obviously referring to the entire Barry family, not one of whom had attended the meetings or any of the fund-raising occasions. The matter was considered resolved, and the priest said that he would approach Joe accordingly, thanked all present for their efforts, and declared the business at an end.

NEGOTIATING WITH NARRATIVE, MOVING TO CONSENSUS

The first point to note about these events is the pivotal part played by the narrative focused on Cathleen and her extended family. The detailed storyline is integral to the way members of the committee, and the wider community from which they are drawn, assess their responsibilities towards a fellow resident. Cathleen herself is Inveresk born: there could

THE GENEROSITY OF COMMUNITY 81

be no question about her identity as 'one of our own'. But the extent to
which she is to be supported is a matter for negotiation, and it is the
information about her family as much as Cathleen herself which becomes
relevant throughout. Gossip in the bars, the shops and the homes, was
undoubtedly important in this, especially in relation to Cathleen's immediate circumstances and those of her five siblings. But the accumulated
details of the comprehensive narrative were more consequential in
provisioning the community with an account of the family's affairs over
an extended period. It was on the strength of this that the decision to
assist Cathleen to the hilt was eventually sustained.

The second point is that this body of knowledge and the sequence of
events of which it was a part drew out, even exposed, the cultural differences between Inveresk people. What was striking about the opening
sequence was how emphatically this was asserted to be business specific
to Inveresk: the women from across the bay were quite clearly excluded.
Subsequently, notwithstanding the priest's attempt to contest his parishioners' parochialism by including Dromore for collection purposes, he
was outmanoeuvred: it was decided by those organising the door-to-door
collection to use children from the National school, none of whom is
drawn from outside the community. Yet despite these developments, this
was also a situation in which cultural differences between village, pier
and country came irrepressibly to the fore.

One illustration of this arose with the proposal that residents should
give either a £10 or £20 note (as distinct from, say, a handful of coins).
Superficially this was rejected on the grounds that pensioners would not
be able to meet this requirement. The real but unstated response from
some of those present was that nobody but a pier person could have
proposed this absurdity in the first instance; it was fully in line with the
stereotype of pier residents being extravagant and wasteful with their
limited cash. After the meeting, I gave a lift to a farmer's wife who
expressed her reaction like this: 'Here they are talking about putting £20
a time in the hat when half the people down there can hardly feed and
clothe their families! I mean, that's just *so typical* of that lot down there.'
Later that night in the packed farmers' house, another country resident
asked of a villager who had been at the meeting the name of the woman
who had put forward the proposal, and when it was given it up, he
commented to much laughter: 'Ah well, that'll be right then, considering
as how that family lives in such luxurious splendour down there!' As all
listening in to the conversation well knew, the family in question were
also mobile home inhabitants.

It will be more than evident, thirdly, that behind this exhibition of
community consensus, a sharp eye was being kept on those not pulling

82   A WORLD OF FINE DIFFERENCE

their weight. Reputations were being undermined as well as enhanced, none more so than those of the Scully and Barry families, both of which came in for sound criticism. For the former, this was nothing unusual. When Inveresk mobilises its resources as a community, more is generally expected from its entrepreneurs than anyone else. But the Scully family as a whole refuses to acknowledge this, as well as other informal rules of conduct; they studiously avoid getting involved in committee work, for example, and they charge a hire fee to local people for use of a small hall in their possession. It was not surprising then that their non-involvement drew forth passing condemnation.

As for the Barry family, what was chiefly confirmed was its total inability 'to pull together' when the occasion conspicuously demanded it. Joseph Barry has already been quoted to the effect that: 'it's as if we're not of the same blood'. As far as those closely monitoring this sequence of events were concerned, there could be no clearer confirmation of that woeful estimation than the way its separate parts stood to one side whilst the community mobilised in Cathleen's favour. As the account should make clear, the final decision concerning the dispensation of the £80 remaining provided an opportunity for people to sanction the Barry family publicly. Although it was Joseph who was to build the wall, it was the family in its entirety which was being condemned for failing to meet up to its moral responsibilities.

In the last analysis, however, notwithstanding the fact that customary divisions of opinion and judgement within Inveresk came to the fore, these were not allowed to subvert in any way the overall process of the community pulling together. Over the brief period of fund-raising, and in the course of its composite events, differences of opinion reflected the entrenched cultural contrasts with which people live on a day-to-day basis. But these were held in check throughout, or they were articulated in the form of witticisms and barbed asides, which were of slight consequence by contrast with the focused way in which the community realised its main goal. As the door-to-door collection got under way, a good percentage of the population was caught up in the wave of enthusiasm generated by the priest and the committee. On every possible occasion, the rhetoric of 'pulling together' and of 'digging deep to help a genuine cause' was extensively expressed, and translated into collective action.

At the end of the day, the most telling consideration was also the most obvious one: the ability of this small community of only 450 adults to raise well over £2000 in about a fortnight was considered to be an outstanding achievement. Although there was no event other than the final committee meeting to bring the affair to a close, there was a palpable if modulated sense of satisfaction that, as one village woman put it: 'We delivered on time, as usual. We did what was expected of us.'

GENEROSITY AND THE SPIRIT OF COMMUNITY

It has to be acknowledged that a degree of self-interest can be involved in responding generously to such appeals for assistance. Some residents recognise they may require similar support too, for there are a number of families in the community who endure similarly difficult circumstances (by 1993, there were still several living in mobile homes, for example). A localised support system is especially needed in a peripheral place like Inveresk, where people are loathe to rely heavily on regional welfare bodies because they so often prove to be impersonal, intrusive, and authoritarian, lacking in any appreciation of the problems of living on a low income in a small place.

In these circumstances, when tragedy strikes in the form of the loss of the head of household's employment, the sudden demise of a spouse, or serious injury to a family member, some form of support from a section of the community often constitutes the most appropriate means of enduring, on-hand assistance for those who have to reorder, in some cases rebuild, their lives. Tragic circumstances can befall anyone, so when people contribute generously to the well-being of others, at least a part-consideration may be acknowledgement that they may face similar circumstances in the future.

For present purposes, however, the theme on which to conclude is that in collective action such as this is exhibited a sense of belonging to the broader community of Inveresk, over and above the particularities of family and domain membership. Whilst there might have been some degree of self-interest involved in contributing to Cathleen's cause, this was much more significantly an emotive response indicative of people's attachment to the community in its entirety. Whatever the extent to which residents' lives are circumscribed by domain affairs, the spatial juxta-position of pier, village and country is such as to encourage, if not force, the residents of each to recognise the broader social unit of which they are a part. I have tried to indicate in the first part of this chapter that there are economic and social relationships which cut across domain boundaries. But most important of all, a huge stock of information about a wide range of other residents, from one end of Inveresk to the other, is available to and is accessed by most residents to some degree. It is in responding and contributing to that stock of knowledge, especially in the interpretation of its prevalent narratives, that a sense of belonging to the whole is inscribed. In symbolic terms, the assistance rendered to Cathleen resonated strongly with that feeling of common membership and shared duty.

More specifically, this collective response was constituted out of a sense of belonging to the whole at the same time as it was constitutive of

84   A WORLD OF FINE DIFFERENCE

that notion of collective membership. Just as the idea of being a member of Inveresk was being tapped into, it was being reproduced and extended also, as indicated by the fact (although not particularly evident at the time) that a new narrative was in the making, one less concerned with the Barry family and more focused on how the community had collectively responded to this moment of crisis. When I returned to Inveresk in 1993, as another long-established resident ran into difficulties (albeit of a lesser order to those of Cathleen Barry), this precedent was invoked to give some direction and legitimacy to the community's possible contribution. There was nothing to preclude the details mentioned about the help rendered to Cathleen being interpreted in different ways, and that narrative being variously deployed as a charter for handling the new crisis. All that was agreed upon, in a sense, was that it was relevant; but precisely how, with what force, and to what end, was something that had to be discoursed about and negotiated over by a quite different combination of community representatives.

It is for these reasons that it seems appropriate to argue that Inveresk's social boundary can be drawn where the stock of detailed knowledge about it expires. As we have seen, Inveresk is wholly integrated into a broader political economy: it has none of the economic or political boundedness which has sometimes been claimed for small communities in Europe. But inasmuch as its residents share a distinct sense of the community as having a boundary with neighbouring communities and the world beyond, it would seem to lodge primarily in the detailed knowledge about it which its residents accumulate and put to use all the time. It is out of the exceptional familiarity which people have of one another, and the uses to which that information is put, that its sense of identity, a sense of its being a distinct and distinctive place in the world, is constituted. This constantly changing stock of knowledge is the unique cultural capital which the residents both produce and consume on a day-to-day basis, and on exceptional occasions also. It is that capital which allows them to exercise to the full the choices which are objectively available to order their small peripheral world as they see fit, including their embarking on acts of striking generosity.

A final contrast may serve to reinforce this argument. Some time after Cathleen had been installed in her new mobile home, the priest sought to capitalise on the same 'community spirit' (his phrase) on behalf of an old woman in Dromore whose house required urgent repair. This woman was known throughout Inveresk, and since her home was inside the priest's parish he pushed the case for assistance in the church and outside it. But the response to this initiative was very poor, because as even long-term Inveresk residents said: 'She's not one of ours', and even 'I don't know the

THE GENEROSITY OF COMMUNITY

woman at all', by which they meant she had no significant part to play in their narrative-replete community discourse.

Consider in comparison the situation of Adi Toolan, who was born and bred in Inveresk and for over forty years has been an energetic member of it. In 1992, her husband died suddenly, Adi herself fell ill, and there were other misfortunes in her family, all of which proved so costly that she announced to her network of friends, drawn from village, country and pier, that she could no longer contemplate going with them on a pilgrimage to Lourdes. The priest indicated that he would try and raise her fare from the community. But even before he had started to properly organise it, donations totalling over £300 were put in his hands, enough to cover Adi Toolan's fare and allow her some cash for the trip as well. Adi was emphatically 'one of us', and the community as a whole was more than ready to say so. Even if the priest was not, the community was quite clear as to where the boundary between Inveresk and the world beyond was to be drawn.

6

FIERCE NEEDLE AND
FINE CRAIC

Although Inveresk folk express on irregular occasions their sense of identification with and moral attachment to the community as a whole, they are also members of associations which articulate Inveresk's identity as a special place on a more regular basis. In this chapter, my concern is to give some sense of what these groups contribute, at different points of time and in different ways, to the idea that this is a distinctive community. Pulling together for a relatively brief stretch with a specific goal in mind is a quite different political exercise from organising an association which lasts for a lengthy period and takes on several objectives. The latter can founder on any number of obstacles, as the history of associations in Inveresk effectively testifies. There is no template which can ensure associational efficacy, which is why the initial requirement is to indicate the variations which exist between groups.

ASSOCIATIONS AND AMBIGUITIES

At any particular moment of time, the number of associations functioning in Inveresk is considerable. In 1983 there were 13, in 1988 there were 10, and in 1993 there were 12. It warrants acknowledgement that there are considerably more in existence nowadays than in the period before rapid social change in the 1960s and 1970s. Whenever I asked older people to compare the current situation with that of the past, opinion consistently had it that formal associational activity had increased substantially. This is open to different types of interpretation, ranging from the fact that nowadays people simply have more time on their hands, to the possibility that this spate of associations is functionally appropriate to sustaining the community's integrity under rapidly changing circumstances.

These groups are always at different stages of development, and they have varied parts to play in the flow of community life. At one end of the spectrum are those groups which have been in existence for a number of years, have contracted in size to no more than a small clique, and which continue to survive only because the remaining members are committed to their particular task. They can be tolerated and even vocally encouraged, provided they neither instruct others what to do, nor make any claim on the community's material and cultural capital.

A good example of this associational type is a small network of half-a-dozen older men and women who are committed to keeping the community as a whole tidy and attractive as well as maintaining public walks along the cliffs. A decade ago, their association had a healthy membership, but over the years it was afflicted by the kinds of tensions described in earlier chapters, as well as mere diminishing enthusiasm, so that nowadays those who remain conduct their affairs as they wish, without any reference to the community at large. For this reason, however, the group can no longer claim much authority within Inveresk, and this limits their contribution considerably. They cannot, for example, impose any pressure to put an end to the frequent dumping of waste over the cliffs, to have the pier cleaned up in preparation for religious ceremonies there, or to get rid of abandoned cars in the vicinity of the terraced houses occupied by pier people.

In recognition of this, the group eventually decided to call a general meeting, the first in several years, in the hope (as one woman put it) of 'recruiting new blood [and] with luck passing on the baton to somebody else – anybody else'. But this widely circulated call for assistance fell on deaf ears: most people held the view that the association's decline had gone too far for any salvage operation to be worthwhile, and it was not long before the small clique resumed its modest efforts to keep in good order at least the more prominent public spaces around the village. The secretary of another association in much the same circumstances as this one expressed their common dilemma like this:

> On the one side, if we try to get things done in the place, people complain that we're always telling them what to do. On the other, if you do nothing, then they'll all say 'Ah ah, there she goes again, just like that Ciara Holland, letting it all go slack again.' You just can't win, but then that's how it goes in Inveresk. And that's how it's always gone.

At the other end of the spectrum are the recently formed groups, full of enthusiasm and good intent, which are generally extensions on current informal networks. For the most part, these are sports groups and they often set their sights on representing the community in regional competitions. One feature of Inveresk which compares strikingly with other rural Irish communities is the relative unimportance of the Gaelic Athletic Association (GAA).[1] One of the reasons for this is that, because of the lie of the land in the vicinity of village and pier as well as the small size of the population, the community has never had its own playing area. Its young men have always had to share facilities with Dromore on the other side of the bay, and as a result, despite the efforts of successive priests (who are usually important to GAA success elsewhere), enthusiasm for this arrangement has always been muted.

At the same time, such sports as football, hurling, fishing and darts have all thrown up enthusiastic teams inside the community, although whether they endure or not frequently rests in the hands of one or two individuals and depends on their effectiveness in generating community support. Some of these, as one might expect, do not last for very long. A darts team, for example, was put together by Alfie Gorman, a local builder who frequented Conor Neeson's bar and was a close friend of Conor's eldest son. The team included regular drinkers who also worked for Alfie, and for several weeks he organised 'training sessions', followed by membership of a minor district league. 'Right lads', he said to the team one evening as it piled into his mini-van to compete in a public house 15 miles away: 'I want you to remember that we're not just in this for ourselves. We're representing Inveresk and we're out to win for Inveresk!' As several games were lost in quick succession, however, and the leading players switched their allegiance to Seamus O'Donnell's team which was doing particularly well, Alfie lost interest quite quickly and the team was disbanded.

By contrast with these unstable, ephemeral groups, there is a small number of more enduring and committed community associations which attend much more seriously to the idea that they are representative of Inveresk as a whole, and work to secure legitimacy within it. Two of these groups will concern us shortly. At this stage the point to be stressed is that all current associations are task specific: they rarely assume goals other than those which generated their formation. Nor do they attempt to amalgamate under some kind of organisational umbrella even when all concerned acknowledge this would be an economical step. The reason given is that anyone who proposed amalgamation would be accused of trying to establish a position of influence over others. The nearest Inveresk has come to this transpired when the newly arrived priest, unimpressed by this associational proliferation, organised what he called 'the community council' under the auspices of which others were expected to function. But its committee members were quickly derided as 'the priest's pets' (or worse), it exercised no wider influence, and the end result was simply to add one more group to those already in existence.

The combined effect of these factors is ambivalence. On the one hand, residents bemoan the lack of cooperation and take it to be symptomatic of the political problems which afflict Inveresk generally. A constant refrain is that 'We can never get to row in the same direction, everybody's always going off in the direction of their own choosing', and this is put down to associations becoming entrenched over time. On the other hand, the fact that there are so many associations is taken as an index of community vitality. Even if residents are not pulling together, there is abundant evidence they are committed to community well-being. As usual, comparisons with neighbouring communities like Dromore and Kilglass are used to highlight that Inveresk is especially active on this score, even if this disguises the point that some associations are not doing much after several years in existence.

The question of representativeness is always pressing for a group which seeks support from residents at large. It becomes all the more so when such associations are enduring and put up major projects. Equally important is the problem of direction and leadership in this egalitarian social field: the ethos of 'every man as good as his neighbour, every woman as good as hers', not only results in protracted meetings but also means decisions are difficult to implement. As a typical meeting unfolds, strict egalitarianism means that everyone who has anything to say has to be allowed to say it. It is also necessary to arrive at decisions through rough-and-ready consensus, not least because any group which is relegated to a minority position through a formal vote may take offence, fission off, and thus subvert the representativeness necessary to realise legitimacy. The contortions which result can be gleaned from a membership poll by one association on a relatively minor matter (the subject of the first question) in which the second question was: 'Will you abide by the decision of the majority: Yes/No?'

Even when consensus has been arrived at, it will not necessarily last for long. Country women especially complain that decisions arrived at after lengthy committee debate get overturned as a result of overnight talk between closer-knit pier and village women. Rather than protest openly about this, they quietly withdraw from committees to which they have been effectively elected as domain spokeswomen. It is elected chairpersons who bear the brunt of such developments, but it is also their responsibility to justify to the community why particular decisions have been taken, why certain goals have been adopted. More difficult still is the cajoling of others into prescribed courses of action without giving any appearance of directing them against their will. If a single generalisation is justified about this complex place, it is that Inveresk folk are unrelentingly against hierarchy. They take the strongest exception to instructions being handed down to them, so any chairperson must exercise considerable skill in implementing even clearly agreed upon proposals.

90 A WORLD OF FINE DIFFERENCE

Any leader in Inveresk, then, has to tread not just one fine line but several. Especially instructive are the difficulties encountered by incumbents of the only two local roles which exercise formally constituted authority, the headmaster of the National school and the priest. Inveresk people recall that in the past these two roles allowed their incumbents considerable power. But this is no longer the case and the results are revealing. The headmaster is a blow-in in his late forties and he has occupied the office for over 15 years. It is acknowledged that he brought extensive enthusiasm to the job, but he is considered to have lost that commitment and become too distanced from Inveresk's ordinary residents. As for the priest, the charge is that he has divided the community by his zeal. He sets in motion too often projects of his own choosing rather than those specified by his parishioners, and his headstrong style has disenchanted those who initially supported his community council. As its chairman eventually said: 'If I say, "Now just hold on a minute Father, let's just sort this out at our own pace", off he'll go with his clique and do it anyway. You just can't do that nowadays. Priests aren't what they used to be. Nor are ordinary folk like me.'

So one figure is accused of doing too little, the other of doing too much. One is considered socially distanced, the other too close to his current clique. There are other problems for both, as we shall see. Neither manages to successfully tread the fine line in which influence is exercised in a manner which meets with community approval. Since considerable authority is still ascribed to these roles, clearly its exercise is going to be all the more problematic when it has to be achieved in the first place by ordinary residents.

PARENTS, PROJECTS
AND PRAGMATISM

An association which generates extensive support and realises significant goals in these circumstances will be well received. In light of the obstacles with which it has come to terms, its success has to be seen as a collective achievement by those who have run it and the community which supported it. Rather more than this, a successful track record by a group which claims to represent the community can be seen as embodying the qualities necessary to sustain Inveresk's integrity in the modern world. In other words, besides being considered in strictly pragmatic terms, it can take on a significant symbolic status as well. In order to amplify these lines of argument ethnographically in this chapter and the next, I turn to the association which came to the forefront of parish politics in 1988, and remained there for the next few years.

FIERCE NEEDLE AND FINE CRAIC 91

It began with a handwritten circular to all parents with children in the National school:

Dear Parents,

A meeting to formally organise a Parents' Association will be held in the School on Wednesday Next March 9th at 8 p.m. sharp. All parents invited to attend. The meeting will also discuss the provision of a Remedial Teacher for the schools in the parish.

Yours sincerely,

Luke McCann.

p.s. please check children's hair and treat if necessary.

At the appointed time, a dozen parents had arrived, along with the headmaster and the priest who was chairman of the school's Board of Management, although he had shown so little interest that it was inoperative. As more parents arrived, he indicated that provision for a Parents' Association had existed for over three years and that this was 'no big thing . . . but it might be useful around now'. According to Department of Education guidelines, the committee could be between six and 22 strong, he said, at which point Con Haughey, a self-employed decorator from the pier, suggested that: 'Eight or so seems about right. You could get a good cross-section with that', to which his married sister, a hairdresser at the pier, added, 'Around eight would get everybody represented all right'.

In line with the unwritten rule not to appear at all 'pushy' (that is to say, forward) on such occasions, as names were proposed excuses were found, until a young mother from the pier allowed her name to stand; three more followed her example. Two of these women then nominated Con Haughey who said he didn't have the time, 'but at least it'll even the numbers up a bit' (by this stage, running at four women to one man). Then two women nominated myself, a village resident, and after miming everyone else's reluctance, I too capitulated. Eventually 12 names out of 31 people present went forward. Since it is another unwritten rule of committee politics that anyone who accepts nomination is also elected (that is, usually there is no election for fear of upsetting anyone who fails to secure a place), the priest said: 'You're all agreed then, these people are the committee. There's no problem here.'

But there was a problem, and it threw the usual routine out of gear. Ann Mulligan, a middle-aged pier resident in the company of three others, asked somewhat aggressively: 'So how does this committee relate to the one set up last year?', a reference to a group assembled ten months earlier to collect signatures for a national campaign against financial cutbacks. The

A WORLD OF FINE DIFFERENCE

headmaster was clearly irritated by this intervention: 'That wasn't a Parents' Association. It never met again after that meeting. This here's the first to get this business off the ground.' Ann Mulligan's close neighbour, Joan Murphy, warmed to the occasion: 'Those who've worked for the school aren't going to like much the way they've been pushed to the side like this'.

She then proposed that the earlier group, none of whom was present, should be coopted onto the committee. The priest and the headmaster objected, and the latter spoke for both of them when he said: 'If those other people wanted to be on the committee, they should have come along. 'Tis not right to put on a committee those who aren't there on the night.' However, Joan Murphy was then supported by her eldest daughter who had married into the Sweeney family: 'These people are going to be fierce upset if they're passed over like this', adding somewhat ominously that her husband would be one such. Con Haughey offered to approach these absent parties 'to see if they'll come in with the rest of us'. This was agreed, as was a proposal to let the committee now make its own way. The priest left, followed by the women who had made their objections known.

After a further round of recalcitrance by all concerned, Con was elected chairman, Ruth Jones (also from the pier) became secretary, and I was elected treasurer. Then the headmaster addressed in detail the topic of the remedial teacher. Several months previously, a divisional schools' inspector had reported that between 20 and 25 per cent of National schoolchildren in the area required remedial teaching before they could effectively progress to secondary education. Another headmaster had proposed an alliance between Parents' Associations in the area to organise some political pressure. This meeting was a belated attempt to ensure input from Inveresk, and after protracted discussion, three committee members (the chairman, the treasurer and a self-employed businessman) were designated to coordinate with the headmaster on this.

By now a good deal had been achieved. Through a neat compromise with disaffected elements, a potentially difficult situation had been avoided. Although the ensuing recruitment of three of these brought the committee to 15 strong (nearly twice the agreed-upon size), it was considered representative: ten women and five men; seven from the pier, four from the village, and four from the country; and there was a wide range of occupations represented too, from full-time housewife and school teacher to waitress and small businessman. Over one third of eligible parents had participated, so it appeared to have a solid constituency.

At a second meeting a fortnight later, the goal was to draw up an agenda. The proposal which proved most revealing by far was the purchasing of a computer which, apart from general use, might prove of value to the remedial teacher once appointed. This was seized upon by

FIERCE NEEDLE AND FINE CRAIC

the chairman: 'It'll be a really progressive move. As the Parents' Association we should be looking toward the future, taking the community along with us. And that's where the future is, in computers.' The question was how to raise the considerable sum of £1200. There were three suggestions: a fund-raising evening with a speaker experienced in the use of computers in schools; a cake and vegetable sale followed by a cabaret at the local hotel; and a 50p levy each week on all households with a child in the school.

At face value, what followed was a straightforward success. Each committee member was allocated five or six households to be visited each week for the 50p levy; most were in the same domain as the member's residence. When the day for the food stall came round, £200 was added to steadily accumulating funds, and a similar sum was realised from the cabaret. Within four months, as treasurer I was able to report that the committee was close to its target.

Behind the scenes, the situation was different. For a start, as time passed the more committee members were called upon to justify in detail what they were doing. The exercise was being closely monitored so that, to draw on my experience, whenever I visited the homes of other village parents, I was rarely able just to collect the levy and depart. I was asked to detail where other finances were coming from, what connections were being exploited to ensure the best purchase deal on a computer, how relations stood within the committee, how much we had already collected, and so forth. There was nothing unusual about my experience.

More telling were the multiple adjustments made in the light of interpersonal relations in different parts of the community. One middle-aged man found it difficult to relate to the country residents from whom he had to collect funds. A product of the pier and trapped in a vicious cycle of unemployment, he felt country folk looked down on him, so he sent his small children to collect the levy, but this resulted in shortfalls. A young mother fell out with two of her pier neighbours, so she arranged for another committee member to call on them instead, even though she was loathe to explain why. Then a male resident in the village encountered such regular complaints from a blow-in household that he abandoned them. None of these adjustments was ever mentioned in committee meetings. But they had to be explained to me as the treasurer keeping a detailed weekly record, this was always done quietly, and it was assumed I would be discreet.[2] In the last-mentioned instance, it was only when my fellow villager and I walked homewards from a meeting, that he explained why, once again, he had just handed in less money than required: 'It's just this one couple who've been cribbing so much, I'm just giving up going. Every time I've been, there's been cribbing about it, so I just got pissed off about it. It's only a young couple but I've just about had it with them.'

Of greatest concern was that around the fourth month of this exercise, certain critical comments were frequent enough to demand attention. Ruth Jones, the committee secretary and a close friend of the woman running the pier shop which is a major source of gossip, dealt with them like this: 'That's it, that's just what this place is like. As soon as anyone tries to do anything progressive, there'll always be the begrudgers. And the only way to deal with them is to bloody well ignore them. They won't go away, but you shouldn't pay them any attention, so.'

But shortly after this, it transpired that the major source of this begrudgery was actually the pier: and not only was the pier contingent on this committee the largest, but some of them also felt that one line of complaint had considerable validity. Con Haughey brought it up at a committee meeting attended by the headmaster. He said: 'The question people are asking is: "How're you, you the teachers I mean, going to make sure all the children get a kind of fair and equal access to the computer?" There's some fierce needle here. They're bothered about total discrimination here, and it's becoming kind of a real issue for some parents.'

It needs to be explained at this point that pier residents have long held the view that National schoolteachers favour children from 'respectable' country and village families at the expense of 'rougher' elements from the pier. This complaint surfaced from time to time; Con was now clearly speaking as a pier resident, not as chairman. When the headmaster feigned a lack of comprehension, he became more forthright: 'Okay, I'll tell you exactly what's being said to me, and it's "Isn't all this going to be for the teachers' pets? Isn't it where the teachers' pets get all the results, and the others just get the crumbs, and that's how it is?" That's what a lot of people near me are saying.' This met with stony silence, until the headmaster replied:

> All I can say to that, Con, is that you're always going to come across a mentality like that one. I've spent a lot of time down over the years collecting money for one thing after another, and I know that as soon as you start, people'll start cribbing, and once it's started it's difficult to stop.

The headmaster's tactic, then, was to ignore this as a complaint specifically from the pier, and to trade instead on the seemingly agreed-upon premise that any 'progressive initiative' will generate a negative response.

ROWING IN THE SAME DIRECTION

The extent of progress on the appointment of a remedial teacher will be addressed in the next chapter. For the moment, it is sufficient to note that developments on that front had stalled entirely whilst the Association itself, especially in its fund-raising capacity, had emerged as a considerable success by mid-year. There were several reasons for this.

First and most important, the committee met up to the expectations of representativeness which were absolutely essential to gleaning community-wide support. Not only did it include male and female residents from pier, village and country, but several of these were also drawn from the more prominent families in each domain; they could be assumed to have full command over its particular discourse. It is never explicitly said on occasions when committees are elected that there must be representatives from each domain. It is simply understood by all concerned that this has to be the case if the committee is going to have any purchase at the level of all of Inveresk. Those involved in the Parents' Association clearly recognised this, both at its inception and subsequently.[3]

Second, a combination of implicit understandings and verbal dexterity was repeatedly deployed 'to keep the committee rowing in the same direction', as a country woman put it. This happened on several occasions, but the exchange described above between the chairman and the headmaster was typical. As a member of a prominent pier family, Con was also that domain's representative, and in that capacity he was duty bound to articulate concerns inside it. He did not mention the pier as such, just 'a lot of people near me', but in the context that phrasing was quite enough: he was being seen to discharge his responsibilities to those around him in the council houses. The headmaster, a country resident, well understood the complaint: he and I had discussed what he termed 'the chip on pier people's shoulders' a few weeks previously. It would have been poor strategy on this occasion to have couched his response in those terms. Instead, with some dexterity, he referred to the difficulties faced by 'all progressives'. But everyone present recognised that Con had made his point, just as all could assume that the schoolmaster had taken proper note of it.

Third, members of the committee invested considerable time in keeping the community informed about the association's progress, and they discussed the community's response between themselves. The importance of this cannot be understated because failure to take these steps in the past has resulted in the collapse of collaborative efforts. Here it was imperative because the education of its young people is a prime community concern, and not just that of parents with children currently in school. Committee members were not surprised to find pronounced interest from the outset: what was striking was the rising level of attention subsequently.

To revert to the terminology of the previous chapter, a new, increasingly involved narrative about the Parents' Association was being constituted, one of equal interest to pier, country and village, albeit in different ways. For some, this became a vehicle for criticising the way the priest and the headmaster conducted school business: how was it, some asked, that a Parents' Association was possible three years earlier but nothing had been done? For others, this was an opportunity for expressing established reservations about teaching personnel. Then again, the idea that this was a 'progressive' step accorded with the self-image of those at the forefront of change in a peripheral setting. If there was a broadly agreed-upon thread to the narrative, however, it was that the association's efficacy indicated how pronounced the commitment to community concerns continued to be. No initiative required this commitment more than improving the resources devoted to the early education of all its children.

Fourth, the committee exhibited throughout flexibility and adaptability, particularly in relation to changing community opinion. It was not just a matter of assessing communal views: there was a dialectical relation between association and community, and this too became part of its ongoing narrative. Following the purchase of the computer, for example, a decision had to be made on the next step. The chairman made his position clear; further fund-raising was needed to purchase new classroom furniture, and his married sister on the committee was of the same mind. Other members privately disagreed, one of them a villager who confided in a pier bar one evening: 'We have to give the whole business a rest for a bit. If we come up with something new again, we're going to put everyone's nose out of joint.' Two pier housewives agreed with this. They would now be 'too embarrassed' to ask for further donations: 'Con is pushing too hard on this money-raising caper. People have had enough for the time being. It's time to give them a break.'

Since fund-raising had effectively become the association's raison d'être by this point, this was a significant difference of opinion and there was some apprehension about the forthcoming meeting. On the day it was scheduled, however, the chairman could not attend because of work commitments, so his deputy, who wanted to call a halt to fund-raising, was in charge. The chairman's sister was running late because of her part-time employment at the pier. As we assembled outside the school, it transpired the deputy chairman had failed to pick up the key to the building from the caretaker.[4] Although everyone knew that each Thursday evening she visited an elderly villager just a few minutes' walk away, no one suggested retrieving the key. Instead the deputy chairman said: 'Well look, there's nothing important that won't wait, right? All we have to do is pay our collection money to our treasurer, and leave it at that, okay?'

All eight committee members who had arrived by this time agreed to this, and after I had made a record of the cash handed in, everyone departed. A major part had again been played by the implicit under-standings central to interaction between those thoroughly familiar with one another. All knew that with the school vacation about to begin, it would be quite some time before another full meeting could be called. Meanwhile, all could be comfortable in the knowledge that an appropriate outcome had been arrived at. Most felt public enthusiasm was diminishing somewhat, it was opportune to call a temporary halt to dipping into the community's pockets, and without any further arrangements having been made, this is what would now happen. But in addition to the committee responding in this way, individual members later made it clear to inquiring parents why they had done so, thus adding a further dimension to the now-substantial narrative which recorded a solid, responsible, and hard won contribution to community well-being.

In sum, efficient and effective associational activity is a political accomplishment which takes into account a number of significant variables. Just as generous assistance will only be rendered to an individual unam-biguously defined as 'one of us', an association which seeks financial support has to be clearly considered 'one of ours'. Whilst the community can be generous in support of worthy causes, any association must be careful in the presentation of these, and how it modifies its activities subsequently. Even bringing an exercise to a conclusion has to be engineered with a firm eye on community-wide opinion, which makes the need for roughly balanced representation as pressing at the conclusion as it is at the beginning. Most important of all, local legitimation is critical precisely because ongoing community investment can be materially and socially expensive; however emotive terms like 'one of ours' might seem, any local association will finally be adjudicated according to its tangible outcomes. This is why even those associations considered the preserve of cliques can be allowed some sliver of legitimacy. Although they have lost much of their influence, they can be acknowledged for the practical contribution they make.

So all associations claiming to work for the public good are weighted in pragmatic, instrumental terms. Inasmuch as a good deal of economic and cultural capital is invested in them, in this down-to-earth social arena their material outcomes are studiously evaluated. But clearly it would be unsatisfactory to reduce the imperative of community to this level alone. A considerable range of anthropological literature on associational activities inside European communities clearly underscores their emotional and expressive dimensions. Some of this literature, to be sure, focuses on areas marked by intense dispute between groups, inter-ethnic conflicts especially, including the collective emotions of people emerging from war-torn contexts: the considerable anthropological literature on Northern

A WORLD OF FINE DIFFERENCE

Ireland is a case in point.[5] But the emotional dimension of community experience is just as important in relatively stable and peripheral small-scale settings such as Inveresk, not least because expressions of emotion both contrast with and complement the emphasis on pragmatism elsewhere.

THE CONCERT AND THE CRAIC

One of the more distinctive expressions of residents' attachment to Inveresk is the craic, those public occasions on which an intensity of shared emotion and well-being is generated in specific places already endowed with a strong sense of belonging.[6] It is in the course of the craic that people's recognition of the importance of Inveresk is underscored, that their sense of attachment to this particular place and its people is highlighted. First and foremost, the craic is collective experience: it is produced on those occasions when residents meet together in order to relax, to be at ease, to entertain themselves, and in the course of doing so they generate a special chemistry which distinguishes certain events from others. It marks them out as occasions to savour and to recall.

This is not to suggest that the craic is a spontaneous eruption of collective well-being: the main reason for focusing shortly on the annual concert is precisely to emphasise that this too is a social achievement based on calculated planning and strategic politics. The craic is unpredictable, though, in that it is difficult to anticipate why certain events generate this pronounced sense of collective well-being when others do not; similarly, whilst two or three events in quick succession might merit the accolade 'fine craic', at other times there may be an extended drought.

These points are best illustrated initially by reference to conventional weekend entertainment when drinking in Inveresk's bars is intense. Especially during the summer months, drinking sessions are noisy, boisterous, entertaining: that much is par for the course. Yet without any kind of notice, the word spreads that the atmosphere in one bar is promising. People begin to drift in its direction, conversation becomes intense, the noise level soars, the arrival of a band generates some singing, there are specific incidents and encounters which add to the rising level of good humour – all of which culminates in an exuberant, enthusiastic, and exhilarating display of camaraderie. At the end of the evening, the craic has been enjoyed by all, but no one can say precisely why in this particular bar on this particular night. There is always a measure of the inestimable which inheres in the craic, and that is its attraction. What remains incontestable is that the performance is collectively produced.

Having made that acknowledgement, there are certain occasions when this overwhelming sense of shared identification and collective well-being

FIERCE NEEDLE AND FINE CRAIC 99

is more likely to transpire than others. St Patrick's Day is one such, not least because copious alcohol consumption is an integral element. Weekends prior to Christmas and the New Year are others; the better-off public houses hold major competitions with substantial prizes, and these generate an especially lively atmosphere. Yet the one event which stands out in Inveresk is quite different from these. This is the annual concert held in the middle of winter in the community hall packed with well over 200 people. Not all concerts are considered successful, and certainly not all generate the craic. But sometimes they do, and this despite the fact that the concert defies some of the informal codes of organisational conduct which other events must abide by if they are to achieve public recognition.

The reason for this lies in the distinctive, indeed unique, identity of the resident in charge, for whilst Jamie Hyde is unquestionably a local in that his parents were from Inveresk and he has never lived elsewhere, he has acquired an unrivalled expertise from over two decades of work outside it. In the late 1970s and 1980s, Jamie led and managed from his home base a highly successful band which travelled throughout the Republic, playing popular disco and dance hall music. In addition to several hit records, the band appeared in many well-known venues as well as on radio and television. This was a local success story in several respects because Jamie's younger brother, Peter, was also in the band, Peter's wife was its lead singer, other musicians were drawn from the immediate area, and the position of road manager was filled by Jamie's elder brother. Over a decade and more, the band became well acquainted with the music scene throughout Ireland and overseas, and they became practised in the changing fashions of popular culture presentation.

As band leader then, Jamie has unrivalled organisational and technical expertise. On the other hand, he has remained (and this is how local people express it too) totally committed to his roots. Because he was born into the pier, he was acquainted with the poverty which prevailed in the 1940s and 1950s since his father was a cobbler. However, unlike the sons who left school to fish with their fathers, Jamie became apprenticed to Peadar O'Donnell, at that time the sole victualler. As a result he became familiar with the culture of country folk because his mentor's supply of meat came from local farmers. When Peadar subsequently bought one of the village's bars and made it into the farmers' house, Jamie took over the butchering trade which located him at the centre of village discourse as well. When Jamie says, then, that he knows everybody in the community 'and everything about everybody as well, much more than they'd sometimes like me to know', this is not an idle boast.

In the course of all this entrepreneurship, Jamie founded the band which, after several false starts, was eventually to transform its members'

100   A WORLD OF FINE DIFFERENCE

circumstances. He and his wife, who is from Dromore, continued to live modestly at the pier alongside his own relatives and also Orla's two sisters who moved into the same domain on marriage. But in the early 1980s, he and his younger brother built expensive residences right on the boundary between village and country. This occasioned widespread comment, but nothing could compromise Jamie's status as a local, not least because he is as firmly wedded to the ethos of family loyalty as it is possible to be. Jamie and Orla have remained in close contact with pier relatives and the gossip to which they are privy, and this they pass on in the blunt language characteristic of pier people.

So when Jamie assumed responsibility for the annual concert, he was able to marry his expertise in popular music and cultural performance with his extensive knowledge of the intricate social field in which the performance was to be situated. In light of his familiarity with interpersonal relations and cultural differences across the community, he was sensitive to the need, for example, to include participants from village, country and pier in more or less equal measure. He once described this to me as 'my annual headache, I know how easy it is to give offence, somehow I've got to find something for everybody to do . . . or else!' The result by the early 1990s was a format which effectively displayed all the talent Inveresk could muster. The concert demonstrably exhibited the pooled endowment of the entire community.

It fell into two parts, the first consisting of a succession of either individual performers or small teams which could be taken to represent symbolically either Inveresk in its entirety or a significant segment of it. Irish dancing is popular in Inveresk – classes are held in the community hall – and it draws together younger and older children from throughout the domains. So following the national anthem, always sung with great pride on such occasions, a dozen immaculately dressed and impeccably drilled young dancers filled the tiny stage. Each was well known, some quickly established eye contact with parents and siblings in the front rows, and once the 15-minute segment was over, it was received with rapturous applause, as well as whistling and cheering from pier youths to the rear of the hall.

This was followed by several solo performers reciting verse or singing ballads. The most striking was Peter Hyde's young son. Dressed in white shirt and black trousers, his hair plastered down across his skull, he proved to have a mesmeric singing voice, the sheer magic of which brought tears to the eyes of older audience members. Then Sandra Scully, a young girl of about the same age from the pier and likewise immaculately attired, began an extended soliloquy in which a young woman debates her future prospects as fiancée, wife and mother. Each stanza ends with the

FIERCE NEEDLE AND FINE CRAIC

exasperated phrase 'Ach, I dunno!', as the narrator equivocates over decisions to be taken at each stage of the life career. The contribution was delivered with such panache and assurance as to generate another sustained round of applause.

This was followed by male teenagers from different parts of the community playing the guitar and drums, and offering passable imitations of well-known rock stars, including Bono and U2. A take-off of Michael Jackson proved especially popular. Then the female peers of these local lads matched their efforts with songs, hairstyles, dress and posturing appropriated from renowned female pop singers like Sinéad O'Connor. Throughout, Jamie provided direction and accompaniment on a small organ from the side of the stage. At this point, the format he had developed entailed members of the professional band making a contribution. On this occasion, as the lights dimmed, Peter Hyde sang a solo melody which he had recently recorded. Many present were evidently familiar with the song, so as the first half of the concert drew to an end, the professional entertainer was accompanied by the young performers who had preceded him, and a substantial proportion of the audience.

The second half also began with solo contributions, including the priest who had abandoned his professional garb to sing the songs of lament favoured by Irish emigrants to the New World. Most had strong chorus lines and the audience was drawn into these. Most of this half was taken up by a lengthy skit written by Orla Hyde. This too had become part of the regular format and it was eagerly anticipated since Orla's talent lay in creating absurd scenarios which involved verbal misunderstandings, cross-dressing, ludicrous deceptions and slapstick, all liberally interspersed with risqué jokes and a few coarse exchanges too.

One of my neighbours, a farmer's wife who deplored such vulgarity in public (and so refused to attend), typified Orla's contributions as 'Benny Hill-type humour', a description which seemed about right to me. But she deftly incorporated elements from the soap opera genre as well as parodies of Irish country life. Her own précis of *The Last Tango* for the evening's programme notes gives some idea of what the 30-minute performance involved: 'Country fever before the end of the week. Three mountainy farmers, a large number of shy and not so shy women, an older daughter husband-crazy, a confused Indian pawn broker. Meet them all at the Ballroom of Romance for *The Last Tango*.' The leading parts were played by Jamie, his younger and older brothers, the headmaster, and a bachelor farmer, along with three young women from the pier and village. All proved enthusiastic performers. Whatever the specifics of the storyline, all was submerged in a stream of slapstick humour, verbal ribaldry, and physical horseplay which brought gales of laughter from the

102 A WORLD OF FINE DIFFERENCE

audience. Finally, after the rendition of a song written by a previous priest about Inveresk's relation to the sea, in which all performers and the audience joined with unrestrained enthusiasm, the evening's entertainment came to an end.

THE POLITICS OF PERFORMANCE

Unlike other communal activities on this scale, the concert was not run by committee but directed by Jamie alone, and as such it was a test of, and a tribute to, his political skills. This is why it was important to first detail his accumulated knowledge of Inveresk and his continuing engagement in it. He was aware of the need to include performers from all three domains: he dealt deftly with interpersonal tensions as these threatened to encroach on the performance; and he knew how to deal with each recruit, both as an individual and according to his or her place in the families and networks which comprise the community as a whole. In *The Last Tango*, for example, it was appropriate for the three attractive young women in search of prosperous husbands (the 'mountainy farmers') to wear somewhat revealing dresses. The mother of one was known for her prudish attitudes, and she began to complain that her daughter's outfit revealed too much. On hearing this, Jamie stepped in quickly. As he described the encounter later (we were in his car on the way to a hurling match), the problem was nipped in the bud:

> Like, I just told her straight that I was in charge of all this, not herself, and what I says goes. So either she shut up about it, and it stayed shut, or Rosie would be off the team altogether . . . And that's what happened because I know that what she likes more than anything is to see her kids up on the stage. 'Cos underneath, she's a bit like that, y'know, she likes to see the family up in the limelight, despite all that crap about appearing prim and proper.

This is not to claim that Jamie was able to keep all disruptive influences at bay. In the performance I have just described, there was a conspicuous absence: one of Inveresk's most talented performers was not in the line up because his father was involved in a major dispute with Jamie's elder brother over the building of a wall between their adjacent properties. The dispute was headed for the circuit court, so this resident determined to withdraw from the concert, at least for the time being. Since his imitations of popular musicians (Elvis Presley, for example) were exceptional, his contribution was missed, and the reasons for it were well known.

In addition to his social skills, Jamie had a level of managerial and technical expertise that no one else could match and it was put to unrivalled success, for what was most telling about the end result was its professional quality. The performers had been trained and drilled to the point at which there were no notably weak contributions or organisational errors. And at all turns, Jamie exploited the opportunity to inject marked symbolic qualities into the production. The deployment of young children as icons of community well-being and vitality was cleverly managed throughout. Every attempt was made to establish a balance between female and male contributions, both as members of teams and as solo performers. In the course of the skit, there were some ingenious role reversals, such as the headmaster performing as a dopey farmer. And there was some inspired casting by Orla Hyde, as when for example a 41-year-old bachelor farmer, in some ways the epitome of country restraint, had to court and canoodle on stage with a 19-year-old woman from the pier. How real or authentic was his awkwardness and embarrassment when confronted with her brash and brazen manner? Were they acting out these cultural differences, or were both behaving as came naturally?

But in addition to its calculated organisational features, there were symbolic properties which could not be as easily reduced to conscious agency. Most especially, there were aspects of the concert performance which were as much a product of the relationship between those on the stage and those in the audience, to the extent that the terminology itself is too clear cut. In all, over 40 members of the community were front stage, whilst about 220 spectators were present on successive nights, and in the cramped space of the community hall, many distinctions dissolved quickly. Whether farmers or fishermen, housewives from the pier or businesswomen from the village, members of long-established families or recent blow-ins, all sat or stood at the rear with scarcely room to move.

Above all, such was the proximity of those on stage to those in the body of the hall that the latter were drawn into the performance and became actively constituent in it. The smiles and winks, the pointing and waving, the whistles and cat calls of encouragement, as well as – most striking and most moving – the way in which the audience joined in the singing led from the stage, all testified to a level of engagement and a degree of identification which was quite beyond organisational contrivance. It was this relation that conspicuously provisioned the performers with a sense of confidence and a degree of assuredness which often contrasted with the sometimes hesitant, occasionally diffident, presentations of individual self in daily life. This audience-induced confidence was reflected in different ways during the evening. Within a few minutes of the supremely assured singing from Jamie's young and usually shy nephew, the audience was involved in a noisy rendition of the latest U2 hit in support of an older teenager recognised as being somewhat quiet and retiring.

104　　　A WORLD OF FINE DIFFERENCE

So on this occasion as with other annual concerts, the local knowledge and professional expertise of Jamie and his close associates, coupled with the enthusiasm and support of the community at large, culminated in a most effective display of Inveresk's reservoir of talent. In song, dance and slapstick humour, the specific abilities of residents from all sections of the community were marshalled into a highly emotional and moving collective endeavour, a collaborative venture of which all were unreservedly proud. The distinct blurring of the performer-audience distinction meant that this could be emotionally savoured as a truly communal effort.

FINE CRAIC AND THE
EMBODIMENT OF COMMUNITY

To this extent, the annual concert is to be seen as a collective representation of the community by the community for its own appreciation, and it is in recognition of this that the appellation fine craic comes into play. This is one of few occasions each year in which, through the efficient mobilisation of its own resources, the community consciously and conspicuously rises above the differences and the divisions which run through it. On other, less immediately impressive occasions, community members practically and persistently mobilise resources and represent Inveresk to the outside world. In the more pedestrian endeavours of the Parents' Association, the residents steadily articulate their commitment in a manner which will ultimately be acknowledged by their fellow locals. But in the narrow confines of the community hall with everyone packed together, laughing at the elementary jokes, joining in a traditional lament, or singing a pop song, one can properly argue that, in this highly emotional moment, the community is representing itself to itself. The image in the mirror is of a community which has an abundance of talent, a sense of unity, and an integrity of purpose which continue to make it a distinctive place in the world.[7]

The work of associations over lengthy periods of time and the concentrated impact of the concert are, then, not just complementary but integrally related under such conditions. The former constitute and then build on the sense of identity which exists across Inveresk through the efforts of those who have preceded them. The process is one of gradual increment, and even that is by no means inevitable, for there are instances of associations dividing the community further, just as specific issues and events have done. But as with the example of the Parents' Association, the contribution can be predominantly positive, and is widely recognised to be so. It is this gradually consolidated sense of belonging which the experience of the annual concert takes distinctly

FIERCE NEEDLE AND FINE CRAIC

further, and this is why it is seen by many as the high point of the community calendar. It is a collective achievement in which the community presents to itself, and then to the world beyond, a united, coherent and distinctive identity. The sense of collective distinction is shared and savoured by those to whom it is supremely important, and this is why it is so often considered *the* night of fine craic.

7

THE POLITICS OF POWERLESSNESS

One of the themes running through this analysis is that, as a modern community, Inveresk is extensively integrated into a broader system of economic regional and global relations which variously impact on its constituent domains. But this uneven process of wider articulation is by no means economic alone. Inveresk is as subject to the influence of hegemonic political institutions, and to the impact of distanced, governmental decision-making processes, as any other modern community, and its inhabitants are well aware of the fact. It is as much part and parcel of their experience of modernity as it is of their sense of peripherality.

In this chapter, one concern is to examine further the symbolic significance of local events like the annual concert. But the other is now to compare the high degree of control which Inveresk people exercise over such activities with the extremely limited influence they have in the broader arena of politics and government. The argument of this chapter is that it is in such experiential contrasts that one finds some explanation for the widespread dissatisfaction with government and politics amongst Inveresk folk generally. On the other hand, such experiences also reinforce at the grassroots the need for local inhabitants to maintain their communal integrity by self-help and collective determination, regardless of the particular place inside Inveresk to which they belong. In other words, they draw the lesson that they have to look to their own interests if the community is to thrive in the future, and that means drawing on the petit bourgeois ethos of self-help and self-reliance which is common to all of Inveresk's three domains.

KEEPING SAMENESS AT BAY

First it is necessary to emphasise the extent to which events on the scale of those described in previous chapters are consciously deliberated upon as collective achievements by those directly involved or just observing from a modest distance. So far, descriptive terms like accomplishment or achievement have been the analyst's, but this is the language of Inveresk people as well, so that when major events like these transpire – I could equally have used, for instance, the details of an annual regatta, the happenings pressed into St Patrick's Day, or even a young fisherman's twenty-first birthday celebration – there is a tangible sense of success in the community at large, a distinct feeling of having, as it were, triumphed against the odds. Inasmuch as vocal, local criticism is often the order of the day, at one level this satisfaction arises from 'humping the begrudgers' (which loosely translates as putting the critics firmly in their place), for there is always some measure of satisfaction in doing that. But the sense of accomplishment is more substantial: it includes above all the recognition that a unified community has been rendered out of its three distinct parts through the residents' own stalwart efforts.

This is not some variation on the argument that a community is a socially constructed affair. It is instead to specify the subjectively felt and subjectively experienced recognition that 'this' community is of 'our' own making, that 'we' have triumphed over the odds in a way that 'other' small Irish communities have not. Inveresk residents do not have to travel far to substantiate the significance of this. The settlement of Kilglass which is nearest to Inveresk (but of which they make negligible use) is a run-down, unattractive and demoralised place in which a comparable sense of pride is lacking. Other small coastal communities have manifestly failed to measure up to changing economic conditions. Further afield still, even in the early 1990s print and electronic media pieces on the death of yet another Irish community were always forthcoming.

So there are various points of external reference which serve to reinforce residents' subjective judgement that they have done well. Owing to their own efforts, the spirit of community palpably, if only occasionally, prevails over the differences and divisions which they have somehow to come to terms with. As a result, what might appear to the visitor as a modest exercise to be taken in one's stride is often seen by Inveresk folk as a major achievement. This is why, to outsiders, Inveresk residents quite often appear (to restate an earlier quotation) 'obsessed altogether with one another'. By comparison with neighbouring communities, this is an especially involved and intricate social world. It is in the coming to terms with this intricacy in discourse, and other forms of social action, that what problematically materialises inside Inveresk appears to an outsider to verge on 'the obsessional'. The view from without simply does not have the same grasp as the view from within on the significance of the cultural variations between the three domains, and the political difficulties which result from them. It is for this reason that the residents of neighbouring communities, as well as some blow-ins who remain on Inveresk's social margins, are so often unsympathetic about the extent to which residents reflect upon and interrogate what they themselves are up to.

To return then to one of the issues raised in the opening chapter, Inveresk residents consider themselves to have thus far kept at bay the prospect of sameness which can threaten, in their view, through the experience of becoming modern as that they have done in recent years. To repeat: by the early 1990s residents held the view that externally located economic, political and cultural forces increasingly pose a cumulative threat to the diversity which they savour, and some of the evidence for this they found in their local material circumstances. In the country, the commodities which a farmer must produce if he is to do well fall within an increasingly narrow range. In the local fishing industry, the types of fish on which a fisherman must concentrate his efforts are more restricted than a few decades ago. Then again, the shops, stores and public houses in Inveresk and the wider region, exhibit little of the diversity which older people recall from their youth. Finally, there is the impact of the mass media on people's everyday lives. Not only does television keep people in the confines of the home, but it is also considered to subject them to the same mind-numbing processes of cultural conformity.

So when Inveresk residents talk about the threat of an externally imposed economic and cultural homogeneity, it is by no means an unreasonable expression of concern. On the other hand, as has been made evident in previous chapters, the threat of sameness can be considered pending rather than present, as it were, imminent rather than in place. But this is owing to their own collective efforts: social diversity persists because, as we have seen, people not only recognise their differences, but they respect them and try to accommodate them at all turns. The pier, the country, and the village are all places of cultural difference in their own way because this is how the residents collectively decide and determine that it should be. The perpetuation of their cultural variability is at least as much a consequence of their own social agency as it is of other influences.

IDENTITY AND INEQUALITY:
THE BROADER POLITICAL FRAMEWORK

There is, however, one sphere of community experience which is considered to remain intractable by contrast with so much else, and this is the sense of powerlessness which most residents share in relation to the wider order of economic and political power. By way of extending the argument introduced in the previous chapter, I want to suggest that there is a relationship between this distinct sense of alienation from the external political order and the commitment which people demonstrate towards keeping alive the spirit of community inside Inveresk.

There is an extensive body of literature which describes the intricate machinery of party politics in the Republic of Ireland.[1] This literature comprehensively addresses such issues as the consolidation of the major parties following the civil war and the establishment of the independent Irish state, the different constituencies subsequently mobilised by the two major parties and the minority Labour Party, the changing ideological emphases of Fine Gael and Fianna Fáil through to the 1950s, and the many changes in party political policies towards the neo-colonial space of Northern Ireland and the post-colonial power of the European Union. To the social anthropologist whose eye remains firmly on grassroots processes, two issues remain unaddressed by this literature. The first is how deeply unacceptable local people consider their encounters with party political and governmental apparatuses to be; the second, which is closely related, is how resentful they are of the broader structures of inequality and power of which these apparatuses are a part.

In relation to the first point, population size is obviously critical: in a small community like Inveresk with a total population of 450 adults, most of whom are anyway fixed in their voting habits, there is little to be gained by a candidate from either of the major parties investing substantial resources to win over new supporters. It may be worth the effort of a newly elected TD (Teachtaire Dála, the elected member of the Republic's lower house, Dáil Éireann) or an aspirant candidate, to do so on occasion. In each instance, the incentive comes from Ireland's distinctive multi-member constituency structure within which weaker, elected candidates can be undermined not only by members of the rival party but also members of their own. But for politicians who are relatively well established in office this is not so pressing, with the result that they can display considerable indifference towards the ordinary voter, who becomes little more than an irritant to be deal with by any means.

Elected TDs, for example, hold clinics in rural constituencies like Inveresk, and ordinary voters attend these to seek assistance in dealing with the welfare bureaucracy, planning departments, the medical system, educational institutions, and so on. They look to the TD to cut through bureaucratic red tape on their behalf. They are rarely seeking to receive any more than their legal entitlement; it is simply that a characteristically tardy process might be speeded up. This is why people find such encounters so unpalatable: they have to dutifully ask the politician's favour, a demeaning performance for people who are remorselessly anti-hierarchical. This is a dimension of clientelist politics which is considered anachronistic in modern times: in Inveresk, people react strongly against it.

They find it especially objectionable because it is always unclear as to whether the politician is indeed providing the service sought, and from time to time, their misgivings are confirmed. In 1993, for example, the shareman on Larry Elliott's boat was his wife's second cousin, Christy Foster. Half way through the year, Christy was imprisoned for seven months for grievous bodily harm following an altercation at a Foxtown nightclub. Immediately he was incarcerated, his family and friendship networks began working for his early release, and this included Carmel Elliott, a staunch Fine Gael supporter who approached the most senior TD in the area. He promised to do all he could by using his personal influence within the judicial system. Christy was actually let out of prison well before he had served the full term, but, for weeks afterwards, his relatives continued to receive a standard letter from the TD's office claiming that he was still working strenuously to secure the young man's release.

The feelings of hierarchy and dependence built into the relation between regional politician and local client are rendered doubly objectionable when such deception is revealed. They compound the sense of powerlessness which begins with numerical insignificance. The second, connected judgement is that those who exercise power from Dublin do so on behalf of those who are already economically and politically powerful. Notwithstanding an abundance of political rhetoric about representing the people, redressing the balance between rich and poor, making the process of politics more accountable, and so on, it is nowadays assumed as a matter of course that the political class is wholly geared to the interests of major Irish corporations and the large transnational companies which dominate key sectors of the Irish economy. Alternatively, it is devoted to maintaining the structural arrangements within the European Union which have proved, since the mid-1970s, such an indispensable source of the capital with which the political class can reproduce its regional power base.

Bearing in mind that Ireland became independent from Britain only in the early twentieth century, and that the nationalist heroes from this period still evoke powerful memories, it is not surprising that ordinary folk resent the way the exercise of political power appears to deepen the

THE POLITICS OF POWERLESSNESS

country's dependence on external, hegemonic powers, as well as reinforcing current inequalities within the society. The abuse of power above and beyond, so to speak, is a matter of constant discussion in Inveresk. It seems that, at all turns, material inequalities are being compounded and that the powerlessness of the majority to whom they belong is inevitable.[2]

The mass media have at least two contributions to make to these grassroots judgements, the first being to expose particular examples of the abuse of power, which some do on a regular basis. In the late 1980s and early 1990s, the outstanding case was the scandal surrounding the Irish beef industry which demonstrated, amongst much else, the extent to which political decision making was driven by the requirements of powerful business interests and their involvement in international trade.[3] The scandal was comprehensively covered, and few could have been left with any other impression but that this was the tip of an iceberg of corruption and abuse involving the public purse. The second contribution has been to articulate what columnists and commentators consider to be variants of public (as distinct from popular) opinion on the behaviour of the political class.

There are several journalists and columnists who are effective on this count, one of whom is the author Nuala O'Faolain whose well-informed diatribes against the political class are enthusiastically read and talked about.[4] In 1988, one such article in *The Irish Times* was headed 'Remember the guys in the smoke filled rooms', and in it she characterised the political class as 'a group of tough gombeenmen . . . (who) . . . recognise each other at a thousand paces' (O'Faolain, 1988). She described them like this:

> They manipulate the local government lists to get their fellow in, adding a name here, moving another to there, playing the locals against head office. They thrive in the smoke filled rooms. They have the stamina of the truly happy . . . They don't give a passing thought to the principles involved in any issue.

Later in the same piece, O'Faolain turned to what many Inveresk residents would consider the heart of the matter:

> And these men are not some interesting but tiny tribe. They are the centre. A concealed centre, they hope: they hope we're all such idiots that we're running around worrying about the nation without even knowing they're there . . . So, keep them in mind always, the guys in the smoke filled rooms. We may have no alternative to being mere electoral fodder to them, but at least we can know it.

The phrase 'mere electoral fodder' well summarises how Inveresk residents assess the part they are allowed in play in the political and governmental processes of Irish society. Their status seems to be one of

112   A WORLD OF FINE DIFFERENCE

enforced subordination, one that allows no recognition, nor any respect. In other words, it is exactly the opposite of how they relate to one another within the limits of Inveresk: it is the very reverse of their acknowledgement of, and compliance with, the implicit, moral codes of interpersonal conduct which people know they have to live by on a day-to-day basis.

As we have seen, within the community everyone is treated as a fully rounded individual: each member has an identity, a status, rights and responsibilities, not only vis-à-vis the extended family but the community at large. When these codes for conduct are departed from, then the defaulter is somehow instructed that is the case; but in most instances, he or she would be aware of having transgressed anyway. In these circumstances, there is no possibility of treating others as if they were other than distinctive social beings. So what local people object to is that, within the political and governmental structures which are supposed to protect them, there is no recognition that they are entitled to respect, to their rights, to be treated with the decency which they routinely accord one another.

The consideration to bear in mind, then, is that those who dominate Irish society are not judged from below as if in some kind of social or moral vacuum. They are judged according to the codes of behaviour which Inveresk people abide by in the course of everyday life, and according to these standards, those who rule from above are found seriously wanting. Note that we return here to the point that social identities are intrinsically comparative, so that just as at the local level the identity of those in one domain is constructed in distinction to that of others, so at a broader level, the identity of the political class, 'them', stands in contradistinction to that of 'us', the ordinary residents of Inveresk. What 'we' are is quite incontrovertibly what 'they' are not; and in these terms, those who rule are to be condemned for their lack of principle, their unbridled pursuit of self-interest, their transparent refusal to treat ordinary people with the respect they deserve.

Inveresk residents do not accept this enforced powerlessness in wholly resigned fashion. There is a small but involved black economy in the community in which numerous scams have been worked out to milk state institutions for all they are worth. The justification for this is that those who rule do the same but on a much larger scale, so what could be amiss with ordinary people taking their share? There are public encounters when every opportunity is taken to lampoon those in power. The skit in the annual concert is an occasional case in point: the rapacious politician (whether county councillor or TD) is ridiculed for his gombeenman qualities. Most frequent of all, there is daily talk in which the latest scandal erupting in the higher echelons of power is made sense of by

THE POLITICS OF POWERLESSNESS 113

virtue of its fitting into a well-established pattern of indifference to principle among those who rule. What such responses have in common, though, is an inability to challenge in any practical fashion the developments which they deride, and this in its turn reinforces the feeling of powerlessness to which they are a response.

This being so, the major lesson to be drawn is straightforward: it is all the more important for Inveresk residents to continue to exercise a high degree of control over the places and the activities of most consequence to them. It becomes all the more imperative that they exercise their innovative abilities to the full in those spheres of local experience in which their individual and collective selves have characteristically found full expression. Inasmuch as there is negligible possibility of exercising any influence in the wider arena of secular politics, local resources have to be marshalled to extract the maximum possible benefit from the social fields with which they are most familiar.

In order to elaborate this comparison in terms which reflect the subjective experiences of Inveresk people, I am going to juxtapose subsequent developments to the two collaborative exercises introduced in the previous chapter. This is not to propose, of course, that this specific comparison was one made by Inveresk residents. It is made heuristically at this point to signal what kinds of contrasting experiences people broadly draw upon when they elaborate the opposition between 'their' world and 'ours', and derive important lessons from such contrasts. For when the sequel to developments within the Parents' Association is set alongside those subsequent to the annual concert, the contrast between the lack of influence in relation to the external secular political system, and the close control exercised over symbolically charged local space emerges with considerable clarity.

SEQUEL ONE

It will be recalled that the need for a remedial teacher was the main reason for instigating the Parents' Association in Inveresk: the divisional inspector had reported that as many as a quarter of National school pupils in the area required remedial instruction. Since this was very much in line with some parents' misgivings about the standard of primary education available to their children, the whole issue generated a good deal of interest in Inveresk. When the time came for the several schools in the area to pool their resources, the Parents' Association representatives were being closely monitored.

The first step was initiated by the headmaster of the National school at Kilglass who called a meeting of all Parents' Association representatives

114   A WORLD OF FINE DIFFERENCE

in the area. Despite an evident caution among some to commit themselves to joint action, he argued it was essential to develop a political strategy which would bring the area's dire need 'to the attention of the powers that be', that is the relevant members of the political class. He proposed they should take advantage of a visit by a junior minister from the Ministry of Education who was already scheduled to open an extension to a Foxtown secondary school. It was also decided to invite the leading TDs and county councillors to this meeting in order to press hard the weight of community concern. Following this, it was proposed to take the matter to Dublin and meet formally with the Minister himself. Establishing a good working relation with his (reputedly very ambitious) junior minister in the first place would be a suitable starting point.

As the meeting convened, it was evident that the priest to whom all National schools in the region were responsible had prepared the ground carefully. Four TDs, three influential councillors, and 16 representatives from the schools were present (including from Inveresk, the headmaster (Luke McCann), its association's chairman (Con Haughey) and treasurer (myself), and Val Egan, another committee member). The junior minister arrived very late with two advisers in tow, whereupon the priest invited the headmaster from Kilglass to present the schools' combined case. He was careful to detail the official findings of the divisional inspector, as well as the extent of concern amongst teaching staff. He concluded: 'We're not asking, Minister, for something we're not entitled to. The official documentation is there. We're just asking for the resources to meet an unquestioned need.' This was more or less repeated by the next two speakers, at which point Luke McCann asked where the parish currently stood on the Ministry list which detailed the ranking of requests for remedial teaching resources. Earlier correspondence with the Ministry of Education confirmed the existence of such a list but it had not revealed the parish's position on it. The Inveresk headmaster said: 'We would like to know, Deputy, how high up we are on the list. We understand we were very high up just a few years back, so can you tell us where we stand now?'

The junior minister, who was in his late thirties, had listened to all this quite impassively. When the priest invited him to reply, he did so with extreme brevity: he understood the parish's concern; many others had the same need; he would keep this submission in mind. Then he stood up as if to depart. He was arrested in his tracks by Luke McCann: those present would appreciate some idea, however imprecise, of the chance of getting a remedial teacher. The junior minister declined to answer this because, he said, he did not know how many teachers would be available in the next school year. Since this was only a few weeks away, the admission came over badly. When another schools' representative emphasised this

THE POLITICS OF POWERLESSNESS

time consideration, and pressed Luke's question further, the junior minister compounded his earlier misjudgement by replying that not only was he unaware of any such current list, but he was unfamiliar with any previous lists, and his tone of voice suggested that he was not especially bothered about them either.

At this point, the TD from a minority party who was well known for his forthright approach, jumped to his feet and accused the junior minister of not knowing the basic facts: 'It's an appalling situation, the Deputy here isn't even in charge of his portfolio, he can't even tell us where we stand on the list'. The remark clearly touched a sensitive nerve because its target angrily retorted: 'I didn't say that, I didn't say that at all, and I didn't come here to get into any cheap political point scoring. I came to listen to you out of good faith, not to get involved in crap of this sort.' Several heated exchanges followed, and with the final throwaway line 'I'm not giving any firm assurances on anything, no assurances whatsoever', the junior minister left the room.

Far from being just an inauspicious beginning, this was also the end of the matter for the foreseeable future. When I left the field five months after this encounter, there was no sign of any remedial teaching, despite the new school year being well under way. More ominous still, whilst official correspondence over this issue had ground to a halt, the National school in Inveresk seemed increasingly likely to lose one of its four full-time teachers because of a slight fall in enrolments. For present purposes, however, the important point is that the relative powerlessness of rural inhabitants was here clearly on display. This was not, it needs to be emphasised, simply the powerlessness of Inveresk. In this instance, several communities were banding together in order to press for a shared, scarce resource, and such an alliance is itself unusual. But what had been quickly made evident was the failure to make an impact, the absence of any negotiation, and above all the lack of authority which the rural residents might bring to bear in an exchange with an influential representative of the political class.

In short, the sense of powerlessness was underscored by this encounter, and as the group drove back to Inveresk a feeling of despair was obvious amongst committee members. Con Haughey commented that 'People back home are going to be sore disappointed with this, now. The association's done well, raising money and all, but this [remedial teaching] was the kind of test case, what it was all about, and we've got nowhere on it, we're all empty handed.' The headmaster concurred with this: 'Well, some of the questions got to him all right, we gave him a bit of a bollocking, so at least he's got the message as to what we're after. But it'll probably all get knocked out of his head on the road back to Dublin.'

116   A WORLD OF FINE DIFFERENCE

Back in the community, the depressing storyline was quickly disseminated amongst concerned residents. As Ruth Jones from the pier put it:

> I mean what's going to happen to the kids who're already behind? They'll just fall behind some more, and I mean that's all wrong. Thing is, it's all so predictable really. There's no Minister, or Deputy, or TD, or whatever, is going to be bothered about a place like this. They're just lining their own pockets while the rest of us, y' know, just keep on going down.

Her comment makes O'Faolain's point about ordinary people being 'mere electoral fodder' in a somewhat different way.

SEQUEL TWO

The organisation of the Parents' Association and that of the annual concert were equally embedded in the fabric of the community: each had to be responsible to community expectations since each claimed to be representative of Inveresk as a whole. But whereas the linkage of the Parents' Association's goals to wider structures of power produced a strikingly negative outcome, the sequel to the annual concert proved different indeed.

In the new year, the entire cast first travelled to the city in order to participate in a government sponsored competition to find the best community-based performance group in the county. Younger members of the cast were enthusiastic about this prospect, and on stage all the performers played their parts with style. What was conspicuously lacking was the unbridled pleasure and overwhelming confidence which had so distinguished the performance in the community hall a few weeks previously. In the large city hall where the competition was held, the substantial audience was drawn from urban and rural communities throughout the county. Those from Inveresk comprised but a tiny proportion, with the result that there could be none of the close association between performers and audience which, I argued, was so critical to creating the sense of a special community event.

In the next month, however, a quite different scenario unfolded unexpectedly. The occasion was the return of the priest who had, in the interim, been transferred to another parish after completing his allotted time in Inveresk. As indicated earlier, his contribution to community life was variously evaluated, but any differences of opinion were now set aside. During his incumbency, he had researched dramatic events at sea (shipwrecks, rescues, and so on) which had involved Inveresk fishermen. Now he was returning to launch his small, privately published booklet on these topics.

For this occasion, the community hall was packed with about 180 people from throughout Inveresk. Immediately, the priest lived up to his

THE POLITICS OF POWERLESSNESS

reputation as a fine raconteur: for over 40 minutes and without notes, he strung together a sequence of anecdotal material which he had gleaned from different sources. 'One occasion, Thomas Barry told me about . . .'. 'Then there was the time I was with John Sweeney . . .'. 'Next, I recall Seamus McGarrity saying to me how . . .'. 'And that fine story from Conor Carty was confirmed for me later by Edward Hyde who . . .' It was a virtuoso performance by a skilled performer who was here communicating (if not also creating) the community's own folklore, weaving diverse threads together into an amusing and entertaining presentation.

When he finally launched his booklet to a round of generous applause, tea, sandwiches and cake were passed around by several women whilst, in the background, a young farmer provided musical accompaniment on his guitar. Then, without any prior notice or evident organisation, an impromptu concert was initiated. The guitarist was unceremoniously ousted, as some pressed others into mounting the stage to repeat their input to the annual concert. There was a slight hesitation until the four men who had been in Orla Hyde's skit mounted the stage, seized the microphone, and produced a song which ridiculed the way council workers drank tea, smoked, chatted, dug a hole only to fill it in again, and devised other ways of avoiding work all day long. The song was ribald, it was sung with gusto, and it had a simple refrain which was quickly picked up by all present.

Scarcely had they finished than several people called out the name of the young boy who had sung so strikingly at the annual concert. Encouraged by a good deal of pushing and shoving from his peers, he mounted the stage, silence fell, and he sang the same ballads as previously, until the refrain of the third drew in all present so effectively that it had to be repeated several times before he dismounted from the stage. His place was taken by the young girl from the pier who had earlier impressed with her recitation, as was the case on this occasion too.

The young farmer with his guitar was given his opportunity to contribute, and then it was the priest's turn to sing the song which celebrates Inveresk's relation to the sea. Everyone knows this song and so it was rendered with spirit, until the priest invited his successor to join him on the stage, and together they sang three Irish ballads which older residents knew well. From this point onwards without any direction or choreography a further six adults and four children made their contribution. Almost two hours were filled with this ad hoc entertainment, until at 11 p.m. the headmaster took the microphone and announced that the priest wished to speak. He indicated that the sale of his booklet had realised over £100 which he was now donating to the community's current fund-raising activities. All applauded and then broke into the

118 A WORLD OF FINE DIFFERENCE

national anthem, and the evening ended on a highly emotional note. This had been a night of fine craic, all the more satisfying because it was unanticipated.

THE POLITICS AND THE
SYMBOLISM OF PERIPHERALITY

On the one hand then, the community's spokespersons encountered a structure of power which reinforced their sense of peripherality and powerlessness. The parish priest had effectively marshalled a range of local and regional advocates to impress on the government's representative the depth of concern about the need for a remedial teacher. The goal was to demonstrate clearly how committed this predominantly rural population was to educational standards at the National school level, and it was, after all, the Department of Education's own systematic study, not a welter of anecdotal evidence, which had provoked this alliance of schoolteachers and parent bodies into collective action.

What was noteworthy about the brief speeches made by community representatives was their careful tone. They were relatively free from rhetoric and emotion. Arguments advanced in the inspector's report were abbreviated, compressed and reasonably presented in order to ensure that, as one of the speaker's put it, 'we keep this discussion on an even keel so that it all works to the children's advantage'. Despite this, the junior minister's response was wholly unaccommodating, and what has to be added is that the political structure of which he was a part is especially rigid and stratified. The stages through which any attempt to access scarce resources must go are clearly demarcated: progress through them is, for the most part, strictly adhered to; and because this is an involved and cumbersome political machinery, the assistance of influential gatekeepers is required at each step. This is why the election of county councillors as well as TDs is followed so closely in rural areas, for it is on such men and women that residents have to rely for assistance as they apply for improvement grants, pensions, health cards, fuel vouchers, and so on.

Inveresk residents certainly find it demeaning to have to go cap in hand to such figures to press for what are mostly legitimate claims. But they realise that some measure of political influence (the ubiquitous 'long leg' of Irish politics) might boost their chances of getting what they deserve and speed up the process. It is necessary, in short, to play the game, and this means being properly deferential to the appropriate gatekeeper. In this particular instance, the relatively influential political figure to whom their pitch was being made evidently saw no advantage to be gained from opening the gate. Putting aside the scarcely disguised arrogance of the

THE POLITICS OF POWERLESSNESS 119

young minister, the structure of power was kept impenetrable by a momentary act, and it was sustained by the even more formidable bureaucratic sloth which marked the ensuing exchange of correspondence between centre and periphery. But by this time, the representatives from Inveresk were wrestling with the even more worrisome prospect of losing a regular teaching position as dictated by the impersonal statistics which determine pupil-teacher ratios.

By way of contrast, the sequel to the annual concert was marked by a spontaneity and a creativity which is only possible between people who are exceptionally familiar with, and respectful to, one another in a place which they consider unequivocally theirs. Of course, one has to recognise that behind what I have termed an impromptu performance lay the many weeks of preparation, planning and practice which went into the annual concert. This was not a performance which materialised out of thin air, but nor was it planned in advance. The momentum of the occasion was created and sustained by the experience and the enthusiasm of the participants themselves.

There was no need for direction for everyone was caught up in the innovative atmosphere generated by the priest as well as the enthusiastic spirit displayed by the four performers who repeated their contribution to the concert skit. What was created once again was the collective spirit which overrides difference and division and which had been so tangible on the night of the annual concert. If anything, the sense of unity was even more pronounced because of that element of spontaneity, which was why in the days that followed the quality of the craic was acknowledged time and again in discourse across the community.

It would clearly be possible to overstate the contrast which I have drawn above. So it is necessary to acknowledge in conclusion that within the next few days and weeks, customary lines of differentiation and division within Inveresk ranks were as pronounced as previously. At least one of the interfamilial disputes discussed in earlier chapters proved quite as disruptive in the conduct of pier life. Inasmuch as I have argued that Inveresk's residents are always subject to different, and by no means complementary, demands on their loyalties and sentiments, one would expect no less. The attachment to community is not (and is unlikely to become) one which consistently supersedes or routinely encompasses other loyalties in this particular context. It is itself a variable factor, one which at certain times and in certain situations exercises slight significance, by comparison with other moments and other occasions in which it is overwhelming in its presence and its symbolic impact.

This is the constant paradox upon which the social life of Inveresk is constructed. There are events which run quite counter to the spirit of

120 A WORLD OF FINE DIFFERENCE

community, significant occasions on which conflicts spin out of control and customary codes of conduct no longer hold. But on the other hand, there are events too in which the sense of pride in belonging to such a distinctive place with its own notions of identity and integrity are clearly elaborated. These are the situations in which the discreet day-to-day work which residents have done in filling the space of Inveresk with meanings of their own making transforms into demonstrable celebrations of pleasure, well-being and a shared identity. They may be momentary and fleeting, but they are no less significant for that.

Yet assuredly the most enduring impression created when events such as the annual concert and the encounter with the government representative are compared with one another, is always going to be that self-help and self-reliance are the indispensable resources to be drawn upon if the community is to look to its own interests and its own future. Despite its having successfully come to terms with modernity, Inveresk remains a peripheral place, economically, culturally, and politically. Not only is it distant from centres of power, but it has none of the cultural distinctiveness valorised by the state on the lines of, for example, the Gaeltacht regions which are able to command substantial government subsidies in order to ensure their sustainability. On all counts, Inveresk's inhabitants have to look to their own interests. Just as individuals and families have had to make sacrifices in the past to consolidate their private property ownership, to pull together in order to get through hard times, and to devise innovative responses to their changing economic circumstances, so the same petit bourgeois dependence on self-sufficiency and self-reliance is recognised to be their most valuable resource if the community is to retain its identity and indeed move forward.

In the last analysis then, the importance of such comparative experiences is to reinforce at the grassroots the ethos which has been imperative to residents in all three domains responding with varying degrees of success to economic modernisation in recent decades. For notwithstanding local lines of differentiation, the widely shared resource of private property ownership coupled with the generalised emphasis on self help have been, as they remain, the source of common sentiments across the community at large. At the core of this is the belief that prospects for improvement always lie at the local level – with the individual and the family, and within the local community, and nowhere else.

The widespread sense of political alienation is a relatively new development inside Inveresk. Until quite recently, memories of the struggle for political independence, the hardship of daily existence until at least the late 1950s, the powerful and engaging nationalism of imposing figures like de Valera, and so on, all worked against recognition of a

THE POLITICS OF POWERLESSNESS

major division between those who ruled and those who were ruled. Nowadays however, the sense of a major class divide between the two categories is widely encountered in Inveresk. But its significance is mainly to reinforce the view that, as ordinary people living in a peripheral place, whatever their particular means of livelihood and place of domicile, it is exclusively their own economic assets, their historical ability to help themselves, and their capacity for mobilising resources for goals of their own choosing, on which the future of the community will depend.

8

CONCLUSION

There is no particular armoury of resources which the residents of Inveresk draw upon to prosecute the politics of identity at the end of the twentieth century. They utilise a wide range of individual talents, organisational expertise and political skills to order their social relations, mount the associations and launch the events which variously articulate a collective identity. Most important of all, they make full use of the copious knowledge which they have about one another to present themselves on occasion as a coherent and moral community. In other words, there is little that is esoteric or exotic about the culture constituted in Inveresk. There are no distinctive ways of cutting turf, no especial rituals connected with drinking, no exceptional marriage relations, and no unique arrangements for dealing with the dead. These may be the stuff of cultural distinction elsewhere on the European periphery, but nothing on these lines is found in this setting.

What this community does have is the kind of internal differentiation and division which many Irish villages and small towns exhibit to some degree. The differences may be more pronounced in Inveresk than places of comparable size: from limited experience elsewhere, my clear impression is that this is the case. But this is nevertheless a matter of degree, and for that reason essentially the politics of Inveresk may not be all that different from the politics of many other places of similar size. What is always important, because it is so inescapable, is that these differences are the source of tension and dispute within particular domains and across the community. Conflict is not put on hold when consensus is being striven for. It is their striking coexistence which establishes what this particular place is all about. It is what gives Inveresk its thick texture as a distinctive place in the world.

CONCLUSION 123

THE AUTHENTIC COMMUNITY?

It is for this reason that Inveresk folk are able to talk about themselves as an authentic community, a modern place which nevertheless exhibits many of the qualities they characteristically associate with community-ness. Anthropologists have, perhaps, been too quick to associate ideas of authenticity with processes of ethnicity: within the discipline, it seems, the authentic community is always an ethnic one.[1] But the sense of being authentic, of exemplifying the attributes and qualities characteristically associated with a particular social form, relationship, or experience, is by no means the monopoly of ethnic groups. It is a recurrent feature in con-temporary experience, and the residents of Inveresk are party to it. They say that theirs is 'a real community' or 'a true community' and this is as much a source of pride as any other element of their collective experience.

The qualification which needs making quickly is that there is no connec-tion between the idea of 'the traditional' and the notion of 'the authentic'. The traditional Irish community is a figment of the anthropological imagination (Peace 1989); it is not part of these residents' cognitive maps. What they mean when they use words like 'true' and 'real' is that Inveresk displays many of the attributes which they and others might historically and contemporaneously understand as constituting community-ness – the centrality of the family, caring for young and old, the combination of intimacy and rivalry, a readiness to help one another, the proliferation of gossip, and so on. There is no particular source from which this construct of the authentic community comes. It is variously assembled from what earlier generations have told them, recollections from their youthful years 30 or 40 years ago, comparable experiences of residence and employment elsewhere in rural Ireland, and even popular cultural representations of Irish life.

But what this typification of authentic experience is emphatically not is romantic or idealistic, for it is as firmly rooted in the practice of everyday life as it is in remembrance of times past. Just as the positive experience of organising for the community's benefit is emphasised, so too is the destructive influence of disputes. The malevolence of gossip is mentioned in the same breath as the intensity of friendships. And the pettiness of many grievances is acknowledged as frequently as expressions of gener-osity. There can be as many painful aspects to living in this intense field of interaction as there are pleasurable ones. Long-established inhabitants say that to live here permanently one must 'learn to take the rough with the smooth, the good with the bad', otherwise one's residence will be marred by disappointment and discomfort. The same is said by now-established blow-ins who, additionally, have had to modify their personal styles of

124 A WORLD OF FINE DIFFERENCE

conduct to fit with prevalent circumstances. Dermot Fitzgibbon is often
cited as a blow-in whose individual style changed quite markedly as he
and his family made the transition from urban-industrial life to a rural
existence. At least in part he is aware of this reputation, although when I
asked him directly how he had managed to survive a rocky introduction
to fishing at the pier, his answer was unequivocal. He had developed, he
said, 'a thick skin, a fucking thick skin'.

At first glance, it might seem paradoxical that it is the blow-in
population and those who have been away for several years who are
amongst the most vocal proponents of Inveresk's authentic character.
The place is inhabited by a number of people who either took up residence
following their alienation from urban-industrial life or returned after
lengthy periods in such metropolises as Birmingham, London, Boston
and Sydney. Whilst some had some success in pursuing careers elsewhere,
a common complaint from their ranks is that they found urban life
dangerous, drug-ridden, noisy, polluted, and (most especially) anomic. One
young pier couple who lasted a mere 12 months in one of the liveliest
suburbs of metropolitan Sydney complained quite openly that they had
made virtually no acquaintances and come to feel 'incredibly lonely'.

Although nothing like as difficult as taking up residence for the first
time, even the experience of re-entry into the flow of Inveresk life has not
been easy for such people, for they have inevitably lost touch with the
details of both domain and community-level discourses, and they have
returned often enough to find that their families occupy quite different
positions to previously in local politics. On the other hand, as indicated
by the fact that they have stayed, they not only savour the more
appealing aspects of residence there, but they are also especially vocal as
to how well it compares with experience elsewhere. They too amplify the
idea that this is an authentic community, but they have the personal
experience of places which are not to back up their judgement. Others are
able to consolidate this by referring to small communities known to them
in Ireland which have likewise undergone modernisation but quite failed
to sustain the qualities of the 'true' community. The construction of several
factories nearby, the development of a ferry terminal, or the transformation
into a commuter suburb, have all been destructive developments for
villages within the wider vicinity. Their experiences testify as to how
successful, relatively speaking, Inveresk has been in becoming modern
whilst remaining a 'real' community in its inhabitants' sense of the word.

CONCLUSION

FROM FIELD TO TEXT

From the mid-1980s to the mid-1990s when the fieldwork for this monograph was done, the discipline of social anthropology was subject to its own transformation, to the extent that some of the topics and emphases which now concern it are quite different from those which prevailed earlier. For a start, the sub-discipline of the anthropology of Europe is now a more important influence, even though the anthropology of Ireland has distinctly diminished in significance.[2] Then again, whilst in the 1980s anthropologists were increasingly encouraged to situate their local studies in relation to regional political economies,[3] at present it is the global system of economic, political and cultural forces which is to be incorporated into the analysis. Further, the social anthropologist has become increasingly obligated to situate herself or himself in the process of moving from the stage of fieldwork encounter to that of writing a monograph. Some of the issues which were debated during this period consumed more attention than was warranted.[4] But before turning in conclusion to what the current study might contribute to an anthropology of Ireland, it is appropriate to specify some of the conditions of its production because the two concerns are interrelated.

The first point is that the organisation of the text bears only limited resemblance to the way in which the ethnographic data was acquired and processed. The monograph is required to be logically ordered, coherently organised and polished in style: all this and more is part of the anthropologist's role as academic artisan. In other disciplines, including some social sciences, such qualities may be characteristic of the data collection process too. But they were not, I acknowledge, applicable to the fieldwork behind this text which was frequently disordered, errant in focus, and far more dependent on serendipitous considerations than could be dealt with here. When one reads other anthropologists' accounts of fieldwork, one cannot but be impressed by the sheer level of control they exercise over the situations in which they find themselves.[5] Some of us, however, have to settle for considerably less, and acknowledge this to be the case.

The second point relates to the first, and reinforces it. My concern throughout has been to examine the meanings of place in the experiential world of Inveresk folk, to quote Feld and Basso again, 'the ways in which people encounter places, perceive them and invest them with significance' (1996: 8), which meant that 'being there' (to use Geertz's (1988) seminal phrase) for extended periods was essential. Yet at least in the course of this study, 'being there' was by no means as straightforward as this elementary phrase suggests. Time and again, the question arose as to where exactly the ethnographer was supposed to be. Was it at the pier, the

126 A WORLD OF FINE DIFFERENCE

village or the country? And if my concern was with the community as a whole, where was the most suitable vantage point for observing and experiencing that? For some while, wherever I was situated significant developments seemed to be taking place elsewhere and I appeared to have been spending time with men who were not 'real fishermen' or with Inveresk residents who were not 'true inhabitants'.

Good fortune was frequently on my side. In the first year of residence, a nineteenth-century dwelling was available on the boundary between the country and the village, in the second a 1930s house became vacant close to the boundary between village and pier, and in the third there was an old cottage for rent on a small farm out in the country. So more by chance than design, I had access to a good cross section of this diverse place through residence alone. But the even-handed account of the three domains in the preceding pages does not reflect a similar equivalence in the field data which I acquired. The pier domain produced far more than either the village or the country, the reasons for which should now be evident: the compact and condensed field of the pier is alive with incidents and happenings on a regular basis. As a result, a day spent fishing and drinking there always produced far more interactional material than, say, in the country where a farmer might speak with no one during his working day, and only with his wife and children in the privacy of the farmhouse early in the morning and late at night.

The third point is that, for most of the time, the ethnographer was also the head of a family of four, sometimes five members strong, so that in certain respects I was a valuable resource in this small place. Not only did I require accommodation, but I also needed provisions, heating, educational facilities, fuel and mechanical repairs, and from time to time medical services as well. Once I had a fair grasp of how commercial arrangements were turned to social advantage by others, I became as able as any other incomer at distributing my custom strategically. Even more important, on the one hand I was able to access the social sites chiefly dominated by Inveresk's men folk, whilst on the other I regularly encountered the natural discourse of local women and children when my family interacted with other families, as we did extensively. Again, there were significant imbalances in the data accumulated over time with, for example, the details of exchanges in public houses being far more prolific than exchanges in shops. But at least the opportunity was regularly there to access the different discourses of women and children. The fact that our three children were at different times educated at the National school was clearly integral to some of the roles I played out. The insight-replete experience of being a committee member of its Parents' Association is only touched upon in chapters 6 and 7.

CONCLUSION

Mention of just two small incidents will underscore how important this role of family head was. On the first, one of my daughters was chatting with two of her secondary school friends over our kitchen table as I was typing up notes from a day's fishing with Larry Elliott and his crew. I was barely listening to their conversation until it suddenly struck me how critically important the daily school bus to Westport was in disseminating gossip from one domain to another, thus contributing to the community-wide distribution of detailed information and the narratives forged from an extensive range of ongoing conversations.

On the second occasion, one of Inveresk's most respectable and respected farming couples accepted an invitation to eat with us. Relaxed and expansive in this family setting, the farmer, who was on the board of the regional cooperative, described how it had been necessary to canvas a broad spectrum of opinion on proposed changes to cooperative policy. It was so important, he said, that 'I went out to every single household in Inveresk to make sure everybody [who would be] affected had a voice. Every single household! I was as organised as a man could be.' I was about to ask whether he meant non-farming households as well as farming ones, when his wife (who was far more community-aware than most country women) saved me from my naïveté by interjecting: 'Of course you didn't, Roland, you didn't do any such thing.' She turned to me: 'What he means is [that] he went to all the farmers' houses, and that was the sum total of it'. Then she turned back to her husband, and scoffed: ' "All the houses in Inveresk," indeed!' It was this incident, and others subsequent to it of course, which drove home how paramount the reality of domain membership – to the unthinking exclusion of all else – can be in Inveresk, and therefore how consistently problematic it is to construct an overarching sense of unity, whether in the course of daily experience or on more exceptional occasions.

The point being driven at here is straightforward but significant. The account of Inveresk presented in these pages is a partial one and a provisional one. Had the ethnographer been, let us say, a single male, or even more pertinently a single female, then the description and analysis would have been different indeed. Had my own circumstances diverged markedly from those sketched above, at the very least the details of the argument would not take their current form or bear their present emphases. In the event, this interpretation is the product of a triangulated relationship over time between the 'I' that I developed as an ethnographer in the field, the multiple identities which Inveresk people presented to one another and which I was privileged to observe over quite lengthy periods, and the 'I' which is my current identity as author of the text. But once this has been acknowledged, it is obligatory for the ethnographer-author to step aside and refocus on the population which is of chief interest.[6]

THE PETIT BOURGEOIS PERSONIFIED?

What then, finally, is the political significance of this small population? And what contribution is being made here to the anthropology of Ireland?

The brief answer to the first question must be in terms of class, and its continuing relevance to the course and complexity of social change in Ireland. It has to be acknowledged that on the whole social anthropology has contributed but marginally to the interpretation of structured inequalities in the Republic, and this, one might propose, is one of the reasons for a decline in its significance over the past decade or so. Despite the unremitting flow of sociological literature on the topic of 'social stratification', the influence of anthropology is barely to be seen, and this has at least two important consequences. As the social structure of Ireland is broken down into the ruling class, the middle class, the working and lumpen classes, and so on, the differences between them are consistently spelled out in terms and according to criteria imposed from above, rather than reflecting the subjectively constituted emphases of the class populations themselves; and the exercise of political agency, in the sense of being able to directly influence the trajectory of social change in Ireland, is reserved exclusively for those who rule.[7] The first weakness testifies to the lack of specifically anthropological interpretations of the differential life worlds and life chances of often fragmented and internally varied subordinate classes; the second testifies to the enormous amount of data about those who rule from the electronic and print media, think tanks, university researchers, and the like.

The central issue is the involved and the intricate complexity of structured inequalities in the Republic today. As with most Western class structures, it is fragmentary, disordered and disaggregated by contrast with the situation a mere 30 years ago, which makes it all the more important that the broad sociological categories of three or four major classes be treated with circumspection. Much closer attention needs to be paid to the details and the specifics of class within this fragmentary and ill-defined structure. Analytic progress will be necessarily slow, and the picture will have to be fleshed out piecemeal. But at least this approach will be more in tune with contemporary complexities rather than riding roughshod over them.

In this light, what are the specific points to be drawn together about the predominantly petit bourgeois population of Inveresk?

First, there is the overwhelming significance of private property ownership, the economic keystone, as it were, that sustains the cultural arch. For whether it is the fisherman who owns his boat, the commercial entrepreneur who owns her shop or public house, or the farmer who

CONCLUSION 129

owns his land and his animals, it is of overwhelming importance that the individual owns the productive resources into which the family invests its labour and thus provides for its needs. The private property owner is the lynchpin of the local economy, his or her enterprise is the pivot of articulation with the wider region, and the owning family is the major unit of consumption as well.

The consequences of this for the identity of the individual and that of the family are far reaching, most especially since it generates a sense of pride and a sense of confidence which are brought to all interactional relations, to the extent that deference is virtually absent from the course of community life. We have seen it to be a maxim of conduct in Inveresk that 'everyone is as good as his (or her) neighbour'. But the relationship between property and people elevates all concerned, as it were, to the same high plane of prestige from which all can feel secure. This population well knows that whilst individual fortunes may fluctuate year by year to the extent that outgoings have to be cut back and sacrifices have to be made, historical precedent is that they will survive through difficult times in a way that others, agricultural labourers and wage-earners for example, have not and this because they do not own their means of livelihood. But in addition to being economically secure by virtue of owning property and being self-employed, the members of this class population are generally assured of a secure status as well.

There is an important qualification to this: property ownership is also a matter of degree, and this is a consideration which recurrently underpins tension and dispute within both domain and community settings. No matter how much private property ownership per se is significant, there are tangible and inescapable differences between the farmer with 125 acres and one with 25, the fisherman with his big boat and one with a punt, and the publican whose business is substantial and thriving and the owner of a shop which is neither. The result is that, however invidious residents might claim the drawing of these distinctions to be, they cannot be consistently ignored, and there is no doubt that the alacrity with which some respond to apparent slights or rebuffs is influenced by such differences. The second important point, however, is that the privileging of private property ownership as such, plus the wide range of cross-cutting ties between all concerned, are factors sufficient to ensure that the ethos of egalitarianism prevails in the great majority of face-to-face encounters.

This is an important point of contrast between the predominantly petit bourgeois rural community and the larger market towns to which places like Inveresk are invariably connected. For in moderate size urban settlements like Bantry, Ennis, and Thomastown,[8] not only would it seem that the significance of class is openly acknowledged, but it is an

130 A WORLD OF FINE DIFFERENCE

important variable influencing the choice of close associates. Class, in other words, is a conspicuous influence in everyday life. This is not the case in Inveresk. It is true, as acknowledged in chapters 3 and 4, that some residents (but not all by any means) will draw a distinction between the community's middle-class and lower-class elements; but this is done on the basis of loosely construed differences in lifestyle, and such comments are always made discreetly. Paradoxically enough, in a prestige-conscious small place like this, all recognise that to be labelled 'class conscious' would be hazardous. This is invariably confirmed when on rare occasion, an outburst of raw anger for example, such a mentality gets exposed: its uncomfortable consequences ramify for a long time afterwards.

The ethos of egalitarianism prevails through a combination of genuine sentiment and calculated compliance, but above all because kinship and friendship ties so persistently and pervasively cut across property owning differentials. Variations in ownership do not just obtain within the community generally: they occur within extended families as well as between close friends, between men and women who have been inseparable since childhood. It will be clear from several chapters that interactional adjustments are constantly being made within family and friendship networks, but changes specifically on the basis of property ownership are few and far between.

If, however, expressions of class difference are absent from this context, to exhibit a sense of pride in what one has achieved as an individual or as a family is entirely acceptable, and indeed to be expected. It is important to reinforce the point that most established property owners in Inveresk have done well out of the last three decades of economic growth, and I have indicated in chapter 2 the variable influence of external forces in this. But it is the ways in which they have themselves seized upon novel opportunities which are of most concern to this petit bourgeois population. It is this which produces and reinforces the emphasis on self-help which is so crucial to individual identity and familial self-esteem.

It is not so much that the influence of the Irish state or the European Community is ignored. It is just regularly understated so that the success of the farmer's, or the fisherman's, or the entrepreneur's career is more in tune with the cultural emphases which predominate amongst petit bourgeois populations generally. It is thus to be expected that those who have succeeded will display pride in their achievements. The only area of contention is how specifically this is done, for some performances can generate a hostile reaction. It will be well evident by this stage that if individuals give the impression they consider themselves superior to others, coming over as especially 'prideful' in interactional settings, then

CONCLUSION

this can trigger strong responses; and in Inveresk, as in any other community, there are a few who are less inclined than most to feel constrained by customary codes of conduct on this score. Some such incidents generate a lot of amusement, and one must never forget that certain types of conflict assume a high entertainment value which is much appreciated, especially if it is at the expense of those who appear pompous and self-important. But other exhibitions of pride go beyond the pale, or get implicated with tensions generated by other factors, and it is at such times that interpersonal and interfamilial hostilities can come to the surface.

So if this profile of a particular fragment of Ireland's petite bourgeoisie has a wider analytic significance, it lies in the methodological imperative to relate private property to matters of identity, status, egalitarianism, self-esteem and pride. Finally, there is the sheer significance of place, for whilst this dispersed, disaggregated and (at least in the view of its membership in Inveresk) disenfranchised population of small to moderate property owners is not, and cannot be, a conspicuous class player on the national political and governmental stage – this can never be a class for itself, in the Marxist sense – the localised place is par excellence the political field in which it can thrive, and it does so through the medium of community identity and integrity.

I have argued throughout that the residents of Inveresk have to be seen as creative, innovative and reflective social actors, and at this stage I would add that, more generally, the anthropology of inequality in Ireland must consider its petite bourgeoisie as active political agents, quite as much as any other class population. What needs especial emphasis, however, is that their material resources, their organisational skills, their interpretive horizons, and their philosophy of self help, are all most effectively deployed in those specific locations with which they are most familiar. Sustaining and reinforcing the identity and the integrity of the particular place of Inveresk makes most effective use of local inhabitants' private material resources and the public knowledge which they have of one another; and it is in the specific and bounded setting too, that they can draw most effectively on the precedents for cooperative effort which are legitimised by narratives of their own construction.

To this extent, the political proclivities of the wider class population are exemplified in the specific locale of Inveresk. A petit bourgeois population is first and foremost a locality focused and a locality bound population, and it is for that reason that any analysis of their distinctive class qualities has to begin with their sense of local place, and arguably end with it as well. The broader significance of this is that, whilst a specific fragment of the rural petite bourgeoisie can (as we have seen) exercise negligible political influence in its own right, the cumulative impact of

132   A WORLD OF FINE DIFFERENCE

this class on Ireland's political culture can be considerable. Over the past two decades, some of the most revealing and divisive national-level debates in Ireland have appeared to be between the powerful 'cosmopolitan' metropolitan core of Dublin, and the 'local' rural communities of the country at large. They have been interpreted as political struggles between the cosmopolitan, progressive elites of the metropolis, and the conservative, local masses out in the rural hinterland. Certainly at one level, the terminology of 'cosmopolitan' and 'local' has some validity. But at another, in substantial part these struggles have been between those who are newly powerful, assertive and growing in confidence at the national level, and those who are newly prosperous, self-confident and self-reliant in local ones. It should not be at all surprising in the light of this study that some of the most important issues contested on these new class lines, for example those relating to divorce and abortion, are ones which turn upon questions of moral conduct and ethical behaviour.

FROM LOCAL TO GLOBAL:
THE END OF IRISH CULTURE?

In their introductory remarks to *Irish Urban Cultures*, Curtin et al. (1993b) outline their charter for the anthropology of Ireland in the following spirited terms:

> We repeat, one of the essential values of anthropology, as a social scientific and humanistic enterprise, is that it provides a view of how people actually live . . . To both chronicle and understand their lives, ethnographers of Ireland should shake off the fetters of their anthropological tradition and training, and immerse themselves in the actualities of an Ireland entering the twenty-first century (1993b: 13).

It should be clear from the preceding pages that I would want to qualify such confident and assured claims: phrases of the order 'how people actually live' and 'the actualities of an Ireland entering the twenty-first century', too readily exclude from view the interpretative authority of the individual ethnographer and the partial, provisional character of the analyses that result from it. Nevertheless, the call is timely and one worth engaging.

The critical issue to be addressed, I propose, is that an anthropology of Ireland may already be difficult to distinguish from an anthropology of the global system. Whilst this is most especially the case with economic and cultural developments in the major metropolitan areas, its bears markedly on ones in the towns and villages as well. One particular phenomenon establishes this point quite unambiguously. Since the fieldwork for this study was completed, the Celtic Tiger burst forth, bringing with it all the

CONCLUSION   133

well-recorded benefits of exceptional economic growth: the creation of
new jobs, improvements in wages and salaries, the expansion of the
building and construction industries, increase in demand for all rural
products as well as imported goods, and the growth of the computer and
popular culture industries. All this and more was celebrated as an Irish
achievement, an economic and cultural renaissance which, driven by the
superfuel of information technology, would transport a prosperous
Ireland well into the twenty-first century.

But once the euphoria generated by the Celtic Tiger abated somewhat
and the rhetoric had run out of ready elaboration, it became clear that
this Tiger was not a Celtic product at all, but the creation of American hi-
tech transnational corporations seeking to consolidate their launch pad
into Europe. The attractions of the Republic ranged from its well-educated
but moderately rewarded labour force through to a 10 per cent rate of
corporate tax. (In Britain, at the time, this stood at over 30 per cent,
whilst in Germany it was 40 per cent.) The presence of American corporations with huge amounts of mobile capital to invest in Ireland is by no
means a recent development, nor is their considerable impact on local
communities.[9] What was striking by the mid-1990s was the sheer scale of
investment.[10] The relevance of these developments here is that the anthropology of Ireland becomes increasingly inseparable from the anthropology
of transnational corporations and the global system which is their arena
of power.

The interface of the local and the global in Ireland opens up two
major prospects for social anthropologists, the first of which is to detail
the impact of the latter on the former, and although in no sense have I
attempted this systematically, some indication of its scale is found in the
preceding pages, commencing obviously enough with the economic
framework in which all social and political action must be situated.
Whether the focus has been small business, fishing or farming, all are
inseparable from the international economic system which establishes
the parameters of power within which localised strategies have to be
worked out. On the side of consumption, the purchase of motor vehicles
from Japan, electrical equipment from continental Europe, foodstuffs
from the United Kingdom and the Iberian Peninsula, and a vast range of
clothing, CDs, videos, magazines and the like from the United States, all
similarly testify to the penetration of the global market into the local
community. Naturally, not all these commodities become resources in the
construction of personal identity, the elaboration of domain difference, or
the celebration of community. But some of them do, and most effectively
so, ranging from prosperous farmers purchasing vehicle types which
reinforce their self-image as respectable, sound and prosperous citizens,

134   A WORLD OF FINE DIFFERENCE

through to the incorporation of American popular culture into the annual concert in such a way as to reinforce the community's image as a modern place which can take in its stride the cultural novelties of the moment.

The second, and in my view more important, prospect is to deploy the findings of local studies as a foil to the pronouncements of macro-theorists on the power of the global system, and here the specific opportunities are considerable. In relation to the present analysis, one possibility is to contest the recurrent argument that the global forces from which the condition of late modernity has been forged have simultaneously transformed local conditions of existence to the point at which ideas of place and attachments to it bear little resemblance, if indeed any, to the experience of previous times. In addition to this, it is argued, the shallowness of any residual attachment to place, coupled with the extraordinary inequalities generated by the contemporary global order, have produced new forms of discontent and alienation amongst increasingly identity-less populations who are unable to compete for the most valued of scarce resources.

Claims of this order are commonplace in the macro-theorising of contemporary sociologists. Certainly it is the case that theorists such as Giddens (1997), Jameson (1986) Lash (1990), Bauman (1999) and Harvey (1989), develop contrasting positions on particular grounds. But Giddens is nevertheless expanding upon a frequently encountered theme when he writes in *The Consequences of Modernity* (1997):

> The primacy of place in pre-modern settings has been largely destroyed by disembedding and time-space distanciation. Place has become phantasmagoric because the structures of means by which it is constituted are no longer locally organized. The local and the global, in other words, have become inextricably intertwined. Feelings of close attachment to or identification with places still persist. But these are themselves disembedded: they do not just express locally based practices and involvements but are shot through with much more distant influences . . . The local community is not a saturated environment of familiar, taken-for-granted meanings, but in some large part a locally-situated expression of distanciated relations. And everyone living in the different locales of modern societies is aware of this (1997: 108–9).

Bauman too has a lot to say about the effects of late modern technology in undermining customary conceptions of space and time, thus affecting the correlate meanings of place and identity. In *Globalization: the Human Consequences* (1998), he summarises as follows:

> For some people it augurs an unprecedented freedom from physical obstacles and unheard of ability to move and act from a distance. For others it portends the impossibility of appropriating and domesticating the locality from which they have little chance of cutting themselves free in

CONCLUSION 135

order to move elsewhere. With 'distances no longer meaning anything', localities, separated by distances, also lose their meanings. This, however, augurs freedom of meaning-creation for some, but portends ascription to meaninglessness for others. Some can now move out of locality – any locality – at will. Others watch helplessly the sole locality they inhabit moving away from their feet (1998: 9).

One of the perennial difficulties of evaluating sociological pronouncements of this order is that one is never quite sure what such gross concepts as 'pre-modern settings' or 'pre-modern states' might be referring to, nor is one ever quite sure what the empirical grounds for issuing such pronouncements are.[11] In place of careful corroboration, there is the commanding voice of an assured intellect: in place of anything so rudimentary as evidence, there is the relentless logic of an abstract argument unfolding from bold premises. All of which makes one hesitate to intervene for fear of being accused of dogged empiricism.

Yet at some point of time, one must feel justified in setting empirical findings against such macro-theories. Contemporary Ireland is, without question, a late modern society. It is fully articulated with the major structures of the world system, including its most advanced technologies: the widespread movement of capital and labour in and out of the country is scarcely a novel development; major cultural innovations in the metropolitan areas exhibit a striking hybridity of regional and global influences; and urban and rural areas alike display the negative consequences of modernity as well. Specifically in the microcosm of Inveresk are concentrated, even crystallised, many of these qualities and attributes – a modern place in a late modern society, but also a distinctly peripheral locale in which, one presumes, the negative effects of global marginalisation should be especially pronounced.

Despite all this, I do not recognise the people I have been describing in this book in the passages quoted from Giddens and Bauman, nor the texts from which they are taken. Local and global influences are assuredly 'intertwined': that much at least seems beyond contention. But can its inhabitants' sense of place be properly described as 'phantasmagoric' in Giddens's sense? Far from locally based practices exhibiting 'much more distant influences' than local ones, I have detailed throughout how the reverse is the case. Then again, if this setting does not qualify as 'a saturated environment of familiar, taken-for-granted meanings', one wonders what kind of place such a description might apply to? As for Bauman's emphases, whilst becoming modern has certainly influenced the extent to which the inhabitants of Inveresk feel marginalised, their locality remains entirely and impressively suffused with meanings, rather than its having lost them. Finally, the sense of helplessness and being out

A WORLD OF FINE DIFFERENCE

of control which Bauman attributes to those who remain wedded to their places of origin (whilst migration, movement, dispersal and freedom become the preserve of those who thrive under late modern conditions) simply does not hold. As we have seen throughout this account, endeavour, self-help and innovation to take full advantage of local and non-local resources in an ever-widening arena of modernisation are the hallmarks of this predominantly petit bourgeois population.

The problem here is not all that dissimilar to that which informs analyses of structured inequality in Ireland: the global system gets sharply, even inexorably, divided into those who have command over the reins of power, establish the direction of societal change, and broadly exercise social agency – those with 'freedom of meaning creation' in Bauman's terms – and those who have none of these qualities and so are condemned to a world of 'meaninglessness' and 'watching helplessly'. It is certainly the case that, as was detailed in chapter 7, the inhabitants of Inveresk share a sense of powerlessness in relation to the politics of government concentrated in the metropolitan core. It is also the case that, following the economic boom of the 1970s and early 1980s, many felt that the economic tide turned against them and that they were made to bear the burden of incompetence, mismanagement and corruption in the upper echelons of power. There is abundant evidence in newspaper reports, magazine articles, electronic media features and opinion polls, that these have become widespread sentiments amongst ordinary Irish women and men. But Inveresk's residents assuredly do not resign themselves to being helpless and ineffectual. Consciously, deliberately, reflectively, they become all the more committed either as domain residents or community members to order their place in the world as they see fit. They may not be successful in some of these efforts: a few may have no impact at all, but that is beside the point. Far from their locality 'moving away from their feet', they remain firmly in command of it and they are proudly aware of the fact.

The modest proposition is, then, that ethnographic studies like this can be used to explore in detail the structures of inequality which prevail in contemporary Ireland. They can also serve to contest macro-theoretical arguments on the condition of late modern society. The two prospects are closely interrelated, and their articulation is important to our comprehending the place of contemporary Ireland in the global system. The requirement common to both is one of detailing how grassroots populations constitute their senses of place, their conceptions of identity, and not only their critiques of broad structures of power but also how they propose to respond to them. In the course of addressing these analytic possibilities, it is clear that certain concepts much used in the anthropology of Ireland hitherto will have to be abandoned, along with the problematic

CONCLUSION

assumptions built into them. Foremost amongst these is the thatched cottage primitivism embedded in the notion of Irish culture, the one concept which has most stood in the way of the anthropology of Ireland keeping abreast of disciplinary developments elsewhere in Europe. If the concept of culture is to be retained, then it has to be reconceptualised in terms of the social and political praxis of everyday life. It is not to be imagined as a hegemonic influence which determines social experience, but instead as the heterogeneity of social practices which emerge as people struggle to bring meaning to the places and the situations in which they find themselves. There is some evidence that this rethinking is under way. The question which arises is how far the processes of twenty-first century globalisation have to go before we are forced to abandon the concept of Irish society as well.

NOTES

1 INTRODUCTION: 'A DIFFERENT PLACE ALTOGETHER'

1 All proper names have been changed throughout this book. At the request of the Committee of the UCD Press, my earlier use of 'Clontarf' for the community has been changed to 'Inveresk', which translates as 'the inlet of the fish'.

2 See Clancy et al. (1986), and Breen et al. (1990).

3 Cohen likewise argues that, whether at the individual or collective level, the sense of self is 'informed by implicit or explicit contrast' (1985: 15).

4 The important point about a social boundary, as Barth points out in his classic statement on the ethnic boundary, is that it

> canalises social life – it entails a frequently quite complex organisation of behaviour and social relations. The identification of another person as a fellow member of an ethnic group implies a sharing of criteria for evaluation and judgement. It thus entails the assumption that the two are fundamentally 'playing the same game', and this means that there is between them a potential for diversification and expansion of their social relationship to cover eventually all different sectors and domains of activity (1969: 15).

5 I hoped to have made this clear in an early paper, Peace (1986).

6 This is the process Basso refers to as 'interanimation' (1996: 55).

7 See also Bender (1993), and Hirsch and O'Hanlon (1995).

8 Here my line of argument echoes that of Cohen who responded some time ago to his own question 'why do communities respond assertively to encroachment upon their boundaries?' with: '. . . One finds in such communities the prospect of change being regarded ominously, as if change inevitably means loss. A frequent and glib description of what is feared may be lost is "way of life"; part of what is meant is the sense of self' (1985: 109).

9 See, for example, the very different perspectives offered by Hannerz (1996) and Friedman (1994).

10 My misgivings are mainly on the grounds that modest ethnographic data is made to carry an exceptional meta-theorising load.

11 This is the strong emphasis given by Cohen (1987) in his study of Whalsay islanders.

NOTES TO PP. 7–17   139

12 See especially Brody (1974), Cresswell (1969) and Scheper-Hughes (1982).
13 For example, Higgins (1984) and Viney (1983).
14 Peace (1989). For somewhat different assessments of the tradition of Irish ethnography, see Wilson (1984), and Taylor (1996).
15 See, for example, the critique of Scottish ethnography offered by Nadel-Klein (1991, 1995).
16 An especially thorough analysis, however, on these lines comes from Salazar (1996).
17 Geertz is here quoting from Casey's essay in the same volume as his own contribution (Casey, 1996).
18 A minimal list of contributions would have to include Cohen (1982, 1986, 1987), Strathern (1981), Byron (1986), Ennew (1980), Nadel (1984, 1986), and Rapport (1993).
19 See, in particular, the critique offered by Knight (1994).
20 This remains the case even when every effort is made to redirect European ethnography away from its villages, as in for example Macdonald (1993).
21 See several contributions to the two volumes edited by Pálsson and Durrenberger (1989, 1996) on the anthropology of Iceland.
22 Macdonald (1993) is a revealing case in point because it demonstrates how, if Ireland is to figure at all, it must be in the guise of Northern Ireland or, better still, in the shape of the province's conflicts in which one can see 'Irish tribalism' at work. The same attitude explains, one suspects, why the two indispensable collections edited by Curtin and Wilson (1989) and Curtin et al. (1993a) appear to have received limited recognition outside the Republic, a response which is virtually anticipated in the introductory remarks to the second of the two volumes.

2 COUNTRY, VILLAGE AND PIER

1 The traditional unit of the townland has no current economic or administrative significance. It is nowadays unusual for a substantial community to occupy a single townland, but broadly speaking the boundary of the one townland matches quite accurately the point at which Inveresk folk consider their community to end and neighbouring ones to begin.
2 The conacre arrangement is particular to Irish agriculture. The designated land is auctioned off to the highest bidder, but only for eleven months of the year. In the twelfth month, it lies fallow, before being auctioned off once again, possibly to the same taker. The fallow period is intended to ensure that the conacre recipient does not come to harbour any ambitious claim to ownership. For an historical interpretation, see Vincent (1995).
3 For an excellent account of the role of women in contemporary Irish agriculture, see O'Hara (1998).
4 The justification for this considerable financial outlay is that otherwise sons would be constantly recruited into helping out on the farm rather than concentrating on their secondary studies.

140 NOTES TO PP. 20–44

5 This is, therefore, a quite different situation from that described for Patricksville by Bax (1976), and for Thomastown by Gulliver and Silverman (1996).

6 Compare this with the arrangements described for Ennis, Co. Clare, by Curtin and Wilson (1989).

7 This line of argument is developed especially in chapter 5.

8 See in particular chapter 6.

9 I have provided a more detailed description of fishing out of Inveresk in Peace (1996).

10 For comparative material, see for example the contributions to Andersen and Wadel (1972), Smith (1977), and Andersen (1979).

11 In comparative terms, what is striking about the social organisation of fishing of Inveresk is the lack of direct involvement by women. Only one fisherman's wife was directly involved in her husband's fishing enterprise, and this was in the preparation of crab and lobster dishes for sale to quality restaurants in the region. This can be compared with the detail of several contributions to Nadel-Klein and Davis (1988).

12 I examine closely the meaning of the term craic in chapter 6.

13 These are the concerns of case studies detailed in chapter 4.

14 My use of such terms as multiplex relations, single-stranded ties, social networks, and the like, broadly follows their usage in Mitchell (1969), but with little of the precision which was required in the heyday of transactional analysis.

3 REGIONAL RELATIONS AND LOCAL IDENTITIES

1 In other words, I am writing here against the increasingly encountered notion that any local level study must examine in great depth the wider economic and political structures which circumscribe it. It is not necessary to discover the wood each time one wishes to describe some of its trees, especially when one recognises that the nature of local-regional articulation is highly variable in its impact at the local level.

2 See Foster (1998: chapter 23).

3 It warrants acknowledgment, however, that this general improvement was modest by comparison with the experience of larger and more powerful farmers in the east of the country as described in the work of Wilson on the 'Euro'-farmers of Co. Meath (1989).

4 This account is based on interviews with regional bank managers, and it bears out the general analysis advanced by Grant and MacNamara (1996).

5 I have described the importance of the salmon season in some detail in Peace (1996).

6 Here I follow some of the useful distinctions spelled out by Sherzer (1987) and Fairclough (1992: chapter 1), but the working definition is my own.

7 Although some current sociological perspectives on micro-contexts would certainly encourage this. In the contributions to Law (1986), for example, the term 'power' gets so stretched as to virtually empty it of meaning.

8 They are discussed at length in this capacity in the next chapter.

NOTES TO PP. 46–73

9 As Mewett writes of nicknames in a Lewis crofting community: 'Nicknames are expressive of both the individual and the social in that each one specifies a particular person in a way that makes it impossible for him or her to be confused with another. Each person, then, is a social person by reference to his nickname' (1982: 238).

10 Also quoted in Feld and Basso (1996: 4).

4 DIFFERENCE AND DISPUTE

1 Curtin rightly points out that 'sociological and anthropological studies of Irish rural communities have largely ignored conflict and disputes' (1988: 76), an omission that he traces back to Arensberg and Kimball's (1968) pioneering work in Co. Clare.

2 I deal with these further in chapter 6.

3 I might add that this is why residents follow the purchasing of new vehicles and the transfer of old ones very closely indeed. It is also why, I would surmise, no two residents ever possess the same make of car in the same colour.

4 Many of these small rituals of community life are perceptively explored in the two early volumes of European ethnography edited by Bailey (1971, 1973).

5 The ethnography of Newfoundland outports has long produced important insights on this order of interpersonal relations. A good deal can still be learned from reading Faris (1966), Szwed (1966) and Wadel (1969, 1979). Gulliver (1996) has likewise described the importance of avoidance strategies in an Irish town in the course of developing a useful distinction between dispute avoidance and conflict avoidance.

5 THE GENEROSITY OF COMMUNITY

1 I deliberately avoid entering the debate over different anthropological approaches to gossip. They have been thoroughly dealt with by Gilmore (1986) in his outstanding study of rural Spain.

2 The proliferation of anthropological literature on narrative forms has been professionally reviewed by Ochs and Capps (1996). The only difficulty I have with their review is their apparent assumption throughout that all narratives must have specific narrators. I am assuming that in Inveresk most residents are significant narrators to some degree or other.

3 A number of social analysts have indeed made the point that narratives are specifically generated in order to deal with the most pressing anxieties currently faced by small groups, or the overt conflicts in which communities are bound up. See for example, Goodwin (1990).

4 This was my rule-of-thumb measure when I had to decide where to cease interviewing farmers and their families at an increasing distance from the hub of the village. As it happened, my judgement more or less coincided with the townland boundary.

142 NOTES TO PP. 73–111

5 Some of the points made in this section have especially benefited from reading Bauman's (1972) seminal paper on the La Have Island general store.

6 In that I single out generosity towards vulnerable others as a major index of community membership, I am struck by the absence of anthropological discussion of generosity in contemporary communities. In the collection entitled *The Ethnography of Moralities* (Howell, 1997), for example, generosity rates only one entry in the index.

7 What follows, therefore, is a highly modified version with a considerable number of 'essential' details omitted or substantially changed.

8 A jolter sells fish from the back of a small trap powered by a donkey or small horse. In 1983, there was one jolter remaining in Inveresk, by 1988 there was none.

6 FIERCE NEEDLE AND FINE CRAIC

1 Bax (1976) is one of the few anthropologists to have recognised the importance of the GAA, especially its connectedness to party politics.

2 Needless to say, I met this expectation to the full, not least because it struck me early on that this was, quite likely, why I had been elected treasurer in the first place. The election of incomers to delicate committee positions in communities like Inveresk is well recorded in the anthropological literature, notably in Frankenberg's classic study *Village on the Border* (1957).

3 The same can be seen to have happened in the election of the committee to help Cathleen and her children, as described in chapter 5.

4 Here, as on a number of occasions, the parallels between my own committee experiences and those of Frankenberg in his Welsh village are strikingly close.

5 Ranging over two decades from, for example, the two contributions by Larsen (1982a, 1982b) through to most recently Bryan (2000).

6 The craic is notably absent from the anthropological literature on Ireland, but this makes it all the more important to rescue it from further debasement on the lines already effected by agencies ranging from Bord Fáilte to Eagleton (1999: 46–8).

7 This metaphorical perspective is especially elaborated by Handelman (1990). In describing the course and content of the annual concert, I have drawn on contributions to Parkin et al. (1996).

7 THE POLITICS OF POWERLESSNESS

1 See, for example, Bew et al. (1989). In this literature, I have always found Carty (1983) insightful. It is certainly the work of a political scientist but nevertheless addresses issues of particular interest to the anthropologist. Coakley and Gallagher (2000) is the most comprehensive of recent texts. For an impressive, if somewhat dated, anthropological approach to local and regional politics in Ireland, see Bax (1976).

2 I am well aware that this sense of powerlessness, or at least collective sentiments somewhat similar to it, are widely encountered in Ireland. Other

NOTES TO PP. 111–135

references to it, however, tend to be fleeting, and this makes it difficult to establish a broader profile.

3 The story is brilliantly told in O'Toole (1995), but much of his account was serialised in *The Irish Times* when the tribunal of inquiry into the beef industry was sitting. The tribunal's findings attracted a huge amount of radio and television coverage as well.

4 Another is O'Toole whose collected essays (1994, 1997) provide some of the most insightful commentary on present-day Irish society.

8 CONCLUSION

1 For some recent examples of this tendency, see the contributions to Cohen (2000).

2 This is acknowledged also in the Introduction to Curtin et al. (1993b). It is interesting to compare this decline with developments over the same period in the rural sociology of Ireland as described by Tovey (1992).

3 This was especially well dealt with in Marcus and Fischer (1986) and also the contributions to Fardon (1990).

4 For a particularly relevant account of the major theoretical developments during this period, see Knauft (1997).

5 The most recent example which comes to mind is that of Rabinow (1999).

6 For a very different emphasis on the role of the ethnographer to the one adopted here, see Varenne's (1993) exploration of suburban life in Dublin 16.

7 See for example the work of Peillon (1982), Breen et al. (1990), and part 2 'Class, Politics and the State' of Clancy et al. (1986).

8 On Bantry, Co. Cork, see Eipper (1986), on Ennis, Co. Clare, see Curtin and Ryan (1989), and on Thomastown, Co. Kilkenny, see Silverman (1989), Silverman and Gulliver (1986) and Gulliver and Silverman (1996).

9 The best account of Irish communities involved in dispute with American transnational companies remains Allen and Jones (1990). For a detailed analysis of one such conflict, see Peace (1997).

10 In 1997 alone, for example, it was calculated at seven billion American dollars,

11 At least in passing, it should be noted that neither of these rather long quotations has any footnotes which might point one in the direction of empirical confirmation. But the same could be equally said about the entire texts from which these paragraphs are drawn.

BIBLIOGRAPHY

Allen, Robert and Tara Jones (1990) *Guests of the Nation: People of Ireland Versus the Multinationals*. London: Earthscan.

Andersen, Raoul (ed.) (1979) *North Atlantic Maritime Cultures: Anthropological Essays on Changing Adaptations*. The Hague: Mouton.

Andersen, Raoul and Cato Wadel (eds) (1972) *North Atlantic Fishermen*. St John's: Institute of Economic and Social Research.

Arensberg, C.A. and S. T. Kimball (1968) *Family and Community in Ireland*. Cambridge, Mass.: Harvard University Press.

Bailey, F.G. (ed.) (1971) *Gifts and Poison: The Politics of Reputation*. Oxford: Blackwell.

Bailey, F.G. (ed.) (1973) *Debate and Compromise: The Politics of Legitimation*. Oxford: Blackwell.

Barth, Fredrik (1969) 'Introduction', pp. 9–38 in Fredrik Barth (ed.), *Ethnic Groups and Boundaries: The Social Organisation of Culture Difference*. Bergen, Oslo: Universitetsforlaget.

Basso, Keith (1996) 'Wisdom Sits in Places: Notes on a Western Apache Landscape', pp. 53–90 in Steven Feld and Keith Basso (eds), *Senses of Place*. Santa Fe, New Mexico: School of American Research Press.

Bauman, Richard (1972) 'The La Have Island General Store: Sociability and Verbal Art in a Nova Scotia Community', *Journal of American Folklore*, 85: 330–43.

Bauman, Zygmunt (1998) *Globalization: The Human Consequences*. Cambridge: Polity.

Bax, Mart (1976) *Harpstrings and Confessions: Machine Style Politics in the Irish Republic*. Amsterdam: van Gorcum.

Bechhofer, Frank and Brian Elliott (1976) 'Persistence and Change: the Petite Bourgeoisie in Industrial Society', *Archives Européenes de Sociologie*, XVII: 74–99.

Bechhofer, Frank and Brian Elliott (1981) 'Petty Property: the Survival of a Moral Economy', pp. 182–200 in Frank Bechhofer and Brian Elliott (eds), *The Petite Bourgeoisie: Comparative Studies of the Uneasy Stratum*. London: Macmillan.

BIBLIOGRAPHY

Bender, Barbara (ed.) (1993) *Landscape: Politics and Perspectives*. Oxford/ Providence: Berg.

Berger, John (1985) *A Fortunate Man*. Harmondsworth: Penguin.

Bew, Paul, Ellen Hazelkorn and Henry Patterson (1989) *The Dynamics of Irish Politics*. London: Lawrence & Wishart.

Boon, James (1982) *Other Tribes, Other Scribes*. Cambridge: Cambridge University Press.

Bourdieu, Pierre (1984) *Distinction: A Social Critique of the Judgement of Taste*. London: Routledge.

Breen, Richard, Damian F. Hannan, David B. Rottman and Christopher T. Whelan (eds) (1990) *Understanding Contemporary Ireland: State, Class and Development in the Republic of Ireland*. London: Macmillan.

Brody, Hugh (1974) *Inishkillane: Change and Decline in the West of Ireland*. Harmondsworth: Penguin.

Bryan, Dominic (2000) *Orange Parades: The Politics of Ritual, Tradition and Control*. London: Pluto.

Byron, Reginald (1986) *Sea Change: A Shetland Society 1970–1979*. St John's: Institute of Social and Economic Research.

Carty, R.K. (1983) *Electoral Politics in Ireland: Party and Parish Pump*. Dingle: Brandon.

Casey, Edward (1996) 'How to Get From Space to Place in a Fairly Short Stretch of Time: Phenomenological Prolegomena', pp. 13–52 in Steven Feld and Keith Basso (eds), *Senses of Place*. Santa Fe, New Mexico: School of American Research Press.

Clancy, Patrick, Sheelagh Drudy, Kathleen Lynch and Liam O'Dowd (eds) (1986) *Ireland: A Sociological Profile*. Dublin: Institute of Public Administration.

Coakley, John and Michael Gallagher (eds) (2000) *Politics in the Republic of Ireland*. London: Routledge.

Cohen, Anthony P. (ed.) (1982) *Belonging: Identity and Social Organisation in British Rural Cultures*. Manchester: Manchester University Press.

Cohen, Anthony P. (1985) *The Symbolic Construction of Community*. Chichester: Horwood.

Cohen, Anthony P. (ed.) (1986) *Symbolising Boundaries: Identity and Diversity in British Cultures*. Manchester: Manchester University Press.

Cohen, Anthony P. (1987) *Whalsay: Symbol, Segment and Boundary in a Shetland Island Community*. Manchester: Manchester University Press.

Cohen, Anthony P. (ed.) (2000) *Signifying Identities: Anthropological Perspectives on Boundaries and Contested Values*. London: Routledge.

Cresswell, Robert (1969) *Une Communauté Rurale de L'Irlande*. Paris: Institut d'Ethnologie, Musée de l'Homme.

Curtin, Chris (1988) 'Social Order, Interpersonal Relations and Disputes in a West of Ireland Community', pp. 76–91 in Mike Tomlinson, Tony Varley and Ciaran McCullough (eds), *Whose Law and Order? Aspects of Crime and Social Control in Irish Society*. Belfast: Sociological Association of Ireland.

Curtin, Chris, Hastings Donnan and Thomas M. Wilson (eds) (1993a) *Irish Urban Cultures*. Belfast: Institute of Irish Studies.

Curtin, Chris, Hastings Donnan and Thomas M. Wilson (1993b) 'Anthropology and Irish Urban Settings', pp. 1–22 in Chris Curtin, Hastings Donnan and Thomas M. Wilson (eds), *Irish Urban Cultures*. Belfast: Institute of Irish Studies.

Curtin, Chris and Colm Ryan (1989) 'Clubs, Pubs and Private Houses in a Clare Town', pp. 128–43 in Chris Curtin and Thomas M. Wilson (eds), *Ireland From Below: Social Change and Irish Communities*. Galway: Galway University Press.

Curtin, Chris and Thomas M. Wilson (eds) (1989) *Ireland From Below: Social Change and Local Communities*. Galway: Galway University Press.

Eagleton, Terry (1999) *The Truth about the Irish*. Dublin: New Island Books.

Eipper, Chris (1986) *The Ruling Trinity: A Community Study of Church, State and Business in Ireland*. Aldershot: Gower.

Ennew, Judith (1980) *The Western Isles Today*. Cambridge: Cambridge University Press.

Fairclough, Norman (1992) *Discourse and Social Change*. London: Longman.

Fardon, Richard (ed.) (1990) *Localizing Strategies: The Regionalization of Ethnographic Accounts*. Edinburgh: Scottish Academy Press.

Faris, James (1966) *Cat Harbour: A Newfoundland Fishing Settlement*. St John's: Institute of Social and Economic Research.

Feld, Steven and Keith Basso (eds) (1996) *Senses of Place*. Santa Fe, New Mexico: School of American Research Press.

Foster, Roy (1998) *Modern Ireland 1600–1972*. Harmondsworth: Allen Lane.

Frankenberg, Ronald (1957) *Village on the Border*. London: Cohen & West.

Friedman, Jonathan (1994) *Cultural Identity and Global Process*. London: Sage.

Geertz, Clifford (1988) *Works and Lives: The Anthropologist as Author*. Stanford: Stanford University Press.

Geertz, Clifford (1996) 'Afterword', pp. 259–62 in Steven Feld and Keith Basso (eds), *Senses of Place*. Santa Fe, New Mexico: School of American Research Press.

Giddens, Anthony (1997) *The Consequences of Modernity*. Cambridge: Polity.

Gilmore, David (1986) *The People of the Plain: Class and Community in Lower Andalusia*. New York: Columbia University Press.

Gluckman, Max (1955) *The Judicial Process among the Barotse of Northern Rhodesia*. Manchester: Manchester University Press.

Goodwin, M. H. (1990) *He-Said-She-Said: Talk as Social Organisation among Black Children*. Bloomington: Indiana University Press.

Grant, Wyn and Anne McNamara (1996) 'The Relationship Between Bankers and Farmers: An Analysis of Britain and Ireland', *Journal of Rural Sociology*, 12 (4): 427–37.

Gulliver, Philip H. (1996) 'On Avoidance', pp. 125–44 in David Parkin, Lionel Caplan and Humphrey Fisher (eds), *The Politics of Cultural Performance*. Providence and Oxford: Berghahn.

Gulliver, Philip H. and Marilyn Silverman (1996) *Merchants and Shopkeepers: An Historical Ethnography of Commerce and Trading in a Southeastern Irish Town 1200–1986*. Toronto: Toronto University Press.

Handelman, Don (1990) *Models and Mirrors: Towards an Anthropology of Cultural Events*. Cambridge: Cambridge University Press.

BIBLIOGRAPHY

Hannerz, Ulf (1996) *Transnational Connections. Culture, People, Places*. London: Routledge.

Harvey, David (1989) *The Condition of Postmodernity: An Enquiry into the Origins of Cultural Change*. Oxford: Basil Blackwell.

Hastrup, Kirsten (1992) 'Writing Ethnography: State of the Art', pp. 116–133 in J. Okely and H. Callaway (eds), *Anthropology and Autobiography*. London: Routledge.

Herzfeld, Michael (1987) *Anthropology Through the Looking Glass*. Cambridge: Cambridge University Press.

Higgins, Michael D. (1984) 'The Tyranny of Images: Aspects of Hidden Control: Literature, Ethnography and Political Commentary in the West of Ireland', *Crane Bag*, 8 (2): 132–42.

Hirsch, Eric and Michael O'Hanlon (eds) (1995) *The Anthropology of Landscape: Perspectives on Space and Place*. Oxford: Clarendon.

Howell, Signe (ed.) (1997) *The Ethnography of Moralities*. London: Routledge.

Jameson, Fredric (1986) *Postmodernism, or the Cultural Logic of Late Capitalism*. Chapel Hill: Duke University Press.

Knauft, B. (1997) 'Theoretical Currents in Late Modern Anthropology', *Cultural Dynamics*, 9 (3): 277–300.

Knight, John (1994) 'Questioning Local Boundaries: a Critique of the "Anthropology of Locality"', *Ethnos*, 59 (3–4): 213–31.

Larsen, Sidsel Saugestad (1982a) 'The Two Sides of the House: Identity and Social Organisation in Kilbroney, Northern Ireland', pp. 131–64 in Anthony P. Cohen (ed.), *Belonging: Identity and Social Organisation in British Rural Cultures*. Manchester: Manchester University Press.

Larsen, Sidsel Saugestad (1982b) 'The Glorious Twelfth: The Politics of Legitimation in Kilbroney', pp. 278–91 in Anthony P. Cohen (ed.), *Belonging: Identity and Social Organisation in British Rural Cultures*. Manchester: Manchester University Press.

Lash, Scott (1990) *Sociology of Postmodernism*. London: Routledge.

Law, John (ed.) (1986) *Power, Action, Belief: a New Sociology of Knowledge*. Sociological Review Monograph no. 32. London: Routledge.

Macdonald, Sharon (ed.) (1993) *Inside European Identities: Ethnography in Western Europe*. Providence/Oxford: Berg.

Marcus, George (1992) 'Past, Present and Emergent Identities: Requirements for Ethnographies of Late Twentieth-Century Modernity Worldwide', pp. 309–30 in Scott Lash and Jonathan Friedman (eds), *Modernity and Identity*. Oxford: Blackwell.

Marcus George and Michael Fischer (1986) *Anthropology as Cultural Critique: An Experimental Moment in the Human Sciences*. Chicago: Chicago University Press.

Mewett, Peter G. (1982) 'Exiles, Nicknames, Social Identities and the Production of Local Consciousness in a Lewis Crofting Community', pp. 222–45 in Anthony P. Cohen (ed.), *Belonging: Identity and Social Organisation in British Rural Cultures*. Manchester: Manchester University Press.

148 A WORLD OF FINE DIFFERENCE

Mitchell, J. Clyde (ed.) (1969) *Social Networks in Urban Situations: Analyses of Personal Relationships in Central African Towns*. Manchester: Manchester University Press/Institute for Social Research, University of Zambia.

Nadel, Jane (1984) 'Stigma and Separation: Pariah Status and Community Persistence in a Scottish Fishing Village', *Ethnology*, 23 (2): 101–15.

Nadel, Jane (1986) 'Burning with the Fire of God: Calvinism and Community in a Scottish Fishing Village', *Ethnology*, 25 (1): 49–60.

Nadel-Klein, Jane (1991) 'Reweaving the Fringe: Localism, Tradition and Representation in British Ethnography', *American Ethnologist*, 18 (3): 500–17.

Nadel-Klein, Jane (1995) 'Occidentalism as a Cottage Industry: Representing the Autochthonous "Other" in British and Irish Rural Studies', pp. 109–34 in James Carrier (ed.), *Occidentalism: Images of the West*. Oxford: Oxford University Press.

Nadel-Klein, Jane and Dona Lee Davis (eds) (1988) *To Work and To Weep: Women in Fishing Communities*. St John's: Institute of Economic and Social Research.

Ochs, Elinor and Lisa Capps (1996) 'Narrating the Self', *Annual Review of Anthropology*, 25: 19–43.

O'Faolain, Nuala (1988) 'Remember the Guys in the Smoke Filled Rooms', *The Irish Times*, 13 June.

O'Hara, Patricia (1998) *Partners in Production? Women, Farm and Family In Ireland*. London: Macmillan.

O'Toole, Fintan (1994) *Black Hole, Green Card: The Disappearance of Ireland*. Dublin: New Island Books.

O'Toole, Fintan (1995) *Meanwhile Back at the Ranch: The Politics of Irish Beef*. London: Vintage.

O'Toole, Fintan (1997) *The Lie of the Land: Irish Identities*. London: Verso.

Pálsson, Gísli (1993) 'Introduction: beyond boundaries', pp. 1–40 in Gísli Pálsson (ed.), *Beyond Boundaries: Understanding, Translation and Anthropological Discourse*. Oxford/Providence: Berg.

Pálsson, Gísli and E. Paul Durrenberger (eds) (1989) *The Anthropology of Iceland*. Iowa: University of Iowa Press.

Pálsson, Gísli and E. Paul Durrenberger (eds) (1996) *Images of Contemporary Iceland*. Iowa: University of Iowa Press.

Parkin, David, Lionel Caplan and Humphrey Fisher (eds) (1996) *The Politics of Cultural Performance*. Providence/Oxford: Berghahn.

Peace, Adrian (1986) '"A Different Place Altogether": Diversity, Unity and Boundary in an Irish Village', pp. 107–22 in Anthony P. Cohen (ed.), *Symbolising Boundaries: Identity and Diversity in British Cultures*. Manchester: Manchester University Press.

Peace, Adrian (1989) 'From Arcadia to Anomie: Critical Notes on the Constitution of Irish Society as an Anthropological Object', *Critique of Anthropology*, IX (1): 89–111.

Peace, Adrian (1996) 'When the Salmon Comes: the Politics of Summer Fishing in an Irish Community', *Journal of Anthropological Research*, 52: 85–106.

BIBLIOGRAPHY

Peace, Adrian (1997) *A Time of Reckoning: The Politics of Discourse in Rural Ireland*. St John's: Institute of Social and Economic Research.

Peillon, Michel (1982) *Contemporary Irish Society*. Dublin: Gill & Macmillan.

Poulantzas, Nicos (1973a) *Political Power and Social Classes*. London: New Left Review Books.

Poulantzas, Nicos (1973b) 'On Social Classes', *New Left Review*, 78: 25–54.

Rabinow, Paul (1977) *Reflections on Fieldwork in Morocco*. Berkeley: University of California Press.

Rabinow, Paul (1999) 'American Moderns: On Sciences and Scientists', pp. 305–34 in George Marcus (ed.), *Critical Anthropology Now*. Santa Fe, New Mexico: School of American Research Press.

Rapport, Nigel (1993) *Diverse World Views in an English Village*. Edinburgh: Edinburgh University Press.

Richardson, Miles (1984) 'Place: Experience and Symbol', *Geoscience and Man*, no. 24. Baton Rouge: Department of Geography and Anthropology, Louisiana State University.

Salazar, Carles (1996) *A Sentimental Economy: Commodity and Community in Rural Ireland*. Oxford/Providence: Berghahn.

Scheper-Hughes, Nancy (1982) *Saints, Scholars and Schizophrenics: Mental Illness in Rural Ireland*. Berkeley: University of California Press.

Scherzer, Joel (1987) 'A Discourse-centred Approach to Language and Culture', *American Anthropologist*, 89 (2): 295–309.

Sennett, Richard (1998) *The Corrosion of Character*. New York/London: W.W. Norton.

Silverman, Marilyn (1989) 'An Urban Place in Rural Ireland: An Historical Ethnography of Domination, 1841–1989', pp. 203–26 in Chris Curtin, Hastings Donnan and Thomas M. Wilson (eds), *Irish Urban Cultures*. Belfast: Institute of Irish Studies.

Silverman, Marilyn and Philip H. Gulliver (1986) *In the Valley of the Nore: A Social History of Thomastown, County Kilkenny 1840–1983*. Dublin: Geography Publications.

Smith, M. Estellie (ed.) (1977) *Those Who Live From the Sea: A Study in Maritime Anthropology*. American Ethnological Society Monograph no. 62. St. Paul: West Publishing Company.

Strathern, Marilyn (1981) *Kinship at the Core: An Anthropology of Elmdon, A Village in North-West Essex in the Nineteen-Sixties*. Cambridge: Cambridge University Press.

Szwed, John F. (1966) *Private Cultures and Public Imagery: Interpersonal Relations in a Newfoundland Peasant Society*. St John's: Institute of Social and Economic Research.

Taylor, Lawrence J. (1996) '"There Are Two Things that People Don't Like to Hear About Themselves": the Anthropology of Ireland and the Irish View of Anthropology', *The South Atlantic Quarterly*, 95 (1): 213–26.

Tovey, Hilary (1992) 'Rural Sociology in Ireland: A Review', *Irish Journal of Sociology*, 2: 96–121.

150 A WORLD OF FINE DIFFERENCE

Varenne, Hervé (1993) 'Dublin 16: Accounts of Suburban Lives', pp. 99–122 in Chris Curtin, Hastings Donnan and Thomas M. Wilson (eds), *Irish Urban Cultures*. Belfast: Institute of Irish Studies.

Vincent, Joan (1995) 'Conacre: A Reevaluation of Irish Custom', pp. 82–93 in Jane Schneider and Rayna Rapp (eds), *Articulating Hidden Histories: Exploring the Influence of Eric R. Wolf*. Berkeley: University of California Press.

Viney, Michael (1983) 'The Yank in the Corner: Why the Ethics of Anthropology are a Worry for Rural Ireland', *The Irish Times*, 6 August.

Wadel, Cato (1969) *Marginal Adaptations and Modernisation in Newfoundland*. St John's: Institute of Social and Economic Research.

Wadel, Cato (1979) 'The Hidden Work of Everyday Life', pp. 365–84 in S. Wallman (ed.), *The Social Anthropology of Work*. ASA Monograph 19. London: Academic Press.

Wilson, Thomas, M. (1984) 'From Clare to Common Market: Perspectives in Irish Ethnography', *Anthropological Quarterly*, 57 (1): 1–14.

Wilson, Thomas M. (1989) 'Large Farms, Local Politics and the International Arena: the Irish Tax Dispute of 1979', *Human Organisation*, 48 (1): 60–70.

Wright, Erik Olin (ed.) (1989) *The Debate on Classes*. London: Verso.

INDEX

alcohol dependence 45, 74, 75
alienation, sense of 11, 109, 110, 112,
    120, 134
Allen, Robert 143 n9
Andersen, Raoul 140 n10
anthropologist, position of 8–9,
    125–7
anthropology 10
  of British communities 7, 9, 139
    n15, 139 n18
  changes in 125
  of global system 133–4
  of Iceland 139 n21
  of Ireland 4, 7, 11, 12, 125, 128,
    131, 132, 136–7, 139 n14,
    142 n6
  of landscape 4
  of place 4, 6
  and symbolic violence 9
  of transnational corporations 133
Arensberg, C. 14 n1
associations 6, 11, 86–90, 97–8,
    104–5
  ambivalence towards 88–9
  differences between 86–8
  emotive qualities of 97–8, 104
  leadership of 89–90
  meetings of 87, 89, 91–3
  numbers of 86
  practical qualities of 97, 104
  representativeness of 89, 91, 92
  symbolic status of 11, 89, 90,
    104–5
  see also Parents' Association
authentic community 123–4
  vs traditional community 123
avoidance strategies 58–9, 102

Bailey, F. G. 141 n4
bailiffs 25, 37, 38, 41
Barry family
  Cathleen (pier resident) 76–85
    assistance to 78–80
    family circumstances 77, 80–1

fire tragedy 76–80
loss of home 76
narrative about 79–80, 80–1,
    83
personal network 77
Joseph (fisherman) 54, 55, 57, 58,
    61, 77, 80, 82
Barth, Fredrik 138 n4
Basso, Keith 4, 15, 125, 138 n6,
    141 n10
Bauman, Richard 142 n5
Bauman, Zygmunt 134, 135, 136
Bax, Mart 140 n5, 142 n1(2)
Bechhofer, Frank 7, 8
'being there' 125
belonging, sense of 6, 22, 29–30, 42,
    43, 46–8, 73, 83–5, 98, 104–5,
    120
Bender, Barbara 138 n7
Berger, John 72
Bew, Paul 142 n1
blow-ins 3, 14, 36, 42, 47, 50, 60,
    62, 63, 74, 90, 93, 103, 108,
    123–4
Boon, James 2, 29
Bord Fáilte (Irish Tourist Board) 142
    n6
Bord Iascaigh Mhara (Sea Fisheries'
    Board) 35, 60
boundary, social 3, 19, 41, 56, 64,
    68, 73, 78, 84, 85, 100, 138
    n4
  and local knowledge 84–5
Bourdieu, Pierre 2
Breen, Richard 138 n2, 143 n7
Brody, Hugh 139 n12
Brown family (the pier)
  in conflict 44, 53–6, 59–66
  James (fisherman) 61
  John (fisherman) 46, 61, 64
  Mickey (fisherman) 53–5
  as 'pure pier' 43–4
  Tadgh (fisherman) 23, 46
Bryan, Dominic 142 n5

152   A WORLD OF FINE DIFFERENCE

business people
   discourse of 39, 40
   failure of 20, 34–5,
   families of 19–21, 23, 41, 44
   money mindedness 21, 34
   relations between 19–21, 29, 34–5,
      40
   resources of 19, 21, 33, 34, 69
   status concerns 20–1, 82
   suppliers of 33–5
Byron, Reginald 139 n18

Cahergal Head 24
Coakley, John 142 n1
Capps, Lisa 141 n2
Carty family (farmers)
   as 'pure country' 43, 44
Carty, R. K. 142 n1
Casey, Edward 8, 139 n17
Catholic church 22
Celtic Tiger 132–3
circuit court 61
Clancy, Patrick 138 n2, 143 n7
class 7–8, 9, 32, 53, 55, 56, 121,
   128–32
codes of conduct 11, 20, 82, 112,
   120, 131
Cohen, A.P. 138 n3, 138 n8, 138 n11,
   139 n18, 143 n1
committees 77–80, 81, 82, 91–3, 94,
   95–8
Common Market/European Union 31,
   32, 33, 35, 110, 130
commons, the 27
community
   council 89, 90
   hall 22, 76, 99, 100, 103, 116
   sense of 4, 11, 67, 75, 107, 109
      and narrative 72–4
   spirit 6, 75, 83–5, 107, 109,
      119–20
   unity in
      obstacles to 28, 49
      organisation of 68, 81, 82,
         83–4, 104, 107
   see also associations
conacre system 16, 139 n2
concert 78, 98
   audience at 103–4, 116–17
   content of 100–2, 112, 134

and craic 98–9, 104–5, 118
   politics of 102–4
   sequel to 116–18, 119–20
   success of 102–3
   symbolic properties of 103, 104,
      106
   and *The Last Tango* 101, 102
conflict 13, 18–19, 26–8, 36–8
   consequences of 62–5
   escalation in 53–5, 57, 59–66
   management of 56–9
   morality of 64–6
   out of control 59–62
Consequences of Modernity, The 134
Coogan family (village and pier)
      53–6, 63
   Elizabeth (housewife) 53, 54, 56, 57
   Dervla 54, 55, 56
   Kevin (fisherman) 53
   Liam (fish buyer) 53, 54, 55, 57
cooperative relations 76–80, 83–5,
      86–90, 91, 105, 113–21
cooperatives 31, 32–3, 127
country, the
   archetypal family of 43–4
   conflict in 18–19
   cultural ethos of 17–19, 64
   economy of 15
   farms in 15–17
   location of 14–5
   see also farming
craic, the 26, 98–9, 104–5, 118, 119,
      142 n6
Cresswell, Robert 139 n12
cultural capital 84, 97
Curtin, Chris 132, 139 n22, 140 n6,
   141 n1, 143 n2, 143 n8

Davis, Dona Lee 140 n11
Dawson family
   Johnny (fish buyer)
   Shiela (accountant)
discourse
   of community 68–9, 70–1, 79, 80,
      85, 124
   defined 38–9, 41
   in domains 22, 38–42, 43, 47, 53,
      62, 68, 99, 124
   and identity 41–3, 45–6
   and knowledge 40, 41

INDEX 153

and marginality 41–2, 47
natural 10, 38, 41, 47, 126
Distinction: A Social Critique of the Judgement of Taste 2
domains 2, 3, 4, 10, 11, 38–42
boundaries between 3, 41
differences between 2–3, 49, 14–30, 63–6
and discourse 38–42, 43, 47–8, 53, 62, 68–70
and individual identity 29, 45–6, 47–8
juxtaposition of 2, 29, 48, 63–4, 83
main qualities of 14–30
as paramount reality 10, 47–8, 127
see also country, pier, village
Donaghue, Donal (fisherman) 75
Dowd, Roland (farmer) 67, 127
drinking patterns 21–2, 25, 42, 44, 45, 56, 58, 65, 70, 75, 98, 99
Dromore 67, 75, 76, 78, 81, 84, 88, 100
Durrenberger, Paul 139 n21

Eagleton, Terry 142 n6
egalitarianism 6, 20, 22–3, 52–3, 55, 89, 129, 130
Eipper, Chris 12, 143 n8
Elliott, Brian 8
Elliott family
Carmel (housewife) 62, 63, 110
Larry (fisherman) 60–6, 67, 73, 110, 127
Ennew, Judith 139 n18
ethnographical tact 8–9
Ethnography of Moralities, The 142 n6
European Union/Common Market 31, 32, 33, 35, 110, 130
experiencing subjects 8, 9
external forces 3, 5, 6, 12, 30, 108, 110–11, 133–4
vis-à-vis business 33–5
vis-à-vis farming 31–2
vis-à-vis fishing 35–8
and local differences 31–9, 46, 106, 108, 113

Fairclough, Norman 140 n6
families
and blood 44–5, 51, 82
in country 15–9, 50
and cousins 51–2
in dispute 27–8, 53–5, 59–63, 77, 79
identities of 43–5, 120–30
and loyalty 17, 28, 49, 50–1, 53, 54, 56, 60, 65
at pier 23, 25–6, 27–8, 50, 51, 53–5
'real kin' 51, 52
typifications of 43–5
in village 19–23, 50, 51
Fardon, Richard 143 n3
Faris, James 141 n5
farmers' house 23, 42, 44, 70, 75, 81, 99
farming
and banks 32–3
and class 32
and the cooperative 31–3
culture of 17–9, 33, 38, 43–4
discourse of 39, 40, 42
families in 15–7, 18, 33, 34, 43, 44, 68
and hard work 17
labour in 16, 17
modernisation of 31–3
organisation of 15–9, 33, 40, 43
and regional relations 31–3, 39
and the state 31–2
see also country
Farrelly, Miriam (businesswoman) 69
Feld, Steven 4, 15, 125, 141 n10
fierce needle 86, 94
fire tragedy 76–80
fish buyers 19, 25, 26, 27, 35–7, 38, 39, 61, 68, 71
competition between 35–6, 41
relations with skippers 35–6, 37
Fischer, Michael 143 n3
fishing 140 n9
conflict in 26–8, 37, 38, 44, 53–6, 57, 59—62
cooperation in 23, 24–6, 37–8
and cooperatives 36, 37
discourse of 39, 40–1, 42, 53, 62, 71

and dole 24, 52
families in 25–6, 43–4, 50, 53–6
market relations of 35–8, 39
narratives of 38
nicknames in 46
relations in 24–5, 26–8, 35–8,
40–1, 53–6
salmon 24, 25, 37, 38, 140 n5
skippers-sharemen relations in 24,
26, 27, 36
types of 23–4
see also skippers, fish buyers
Fitzgibbon family 70, 71
Dermot (fisherman) 58, 70, 71,
124
Flaherty, Donal (victualler) 20
Foley, Charlie (boat mechanic) 40
Foster, Christy (fisherman) 110
Foster, Roy 140 n2
Foxtown 34, 40, 57, 77, 114
Frankenberg, Ronald 142 n2 and 4
Free State 46
Friedman, Jonathan 138 n9

Gaelic Athletic Association (GAA) 87
Gaeltacht regions 120
Gallagher, Michael 142 n1
Geertz, Clifford 8, 9, 125, 139 n17
generosity 67, 68, 74, 123
and community spirit 82–5
and narrative 74–6
Geoghagen, Dickie (fisherman) 38
Giddens, Anthony 134, 135
Gilmore, David, 141 n1
global system 10, 133, 134, 136
processes of 5, 10
*Globalization: the Human
Consequences* 134
Goodwin, M.H. 141 n3
Gorman, Alfie (builder) 88
gossip 11, 23, 56, 74, 123, 127
and narrative 11, 72–3, 81
defined 72
Grant, Wyn 140 n4
Gulliver, Philip H. 140 n5, 141 n5,
143 n8

Handelman, Don 142 n7
Hannerz, Ulf 138 n9
Hastrup, Kirsten 9

Haughey, Con (decorator) 91, 92, 94,
95, 96, 114, 115
'hanging around' 8, 9
Harvey, David 134
headmaster 23, 90, 91, 94, 95, 96,
101, 103, 114, 115, 117
Herzfeld, Michael 9
Higgins, Colm (schoolteacher) 42
Higgins, Michael D. 139 n13
High Court 61–2, 64–5
Hirsch, Eric 138 n7
household kitchen 71
Howell, Signe 142 n6
Hyde family (pier and village) 50
Jamie (musician)
background 99–100
and concert 100–2
political skills 102–4
Orla (scriptwriter) 100, 101, 117
Peter (musician) 99, 100, 101

identity
and belonging 42, 46–8, 84–5
and blood 44–5
and difference 2
family 43–5, 129–30
individual 29, 43, 45–6, 47–8,
112, 113, 129–30, 133
and place 4, 8, 10, 12, 15, 28,
29–30, 42–8, 84, 113
and property 8, 17, 46, 130
Inveresk
associations in 6, 11, 86–90, 91–2,
97–8, 104–5
black economy 112
changes in 1, 11, 12, 15, 16, 20,
31–3, 34–5, 74, 120, 130
class in 7, 32, 53, 55, 128–31
codes of behaviour in 2, 20, 82,
112, 120, 131
conflict in 11, 13, 18–9, 26–8, 44,
57, 59–66, 112, 122
cooperation in 40, 76–80, 83–5,
86, 90, 91–105, 113–21
cross–cutting ties in 68–9
differences within 1–5, 6, 7, 10–1,
28–30, 31–8, 41, 81–2, 108,
122
domains in 2, 3, 4, 10, 14–30,
38–42, 47, 55, 57, 63–4, 108

INDEX

155

(*see also* country, village, pier)
drinking in 21–2, 25, 44, 45, 56,
  58, 65, 70, 75, 98–9
economy of 1,15–7, 19–23, 24–7,
  31–8, 68–9
(*see also* farming, fishing, business)
egalitarianism in 6, 20–3, 52–3,
  55, 89, 129–30
entrepreneurship in 5, 19–23,
  33–4, 35–7, 68–9, 120–1
future of 5, 120–1
gossip in 11, 23, 56, 72–3, 74, 81,
  123, 127
leadership in 6, 11, 89–90
and modernisation 1, 5, 31, 106,
  120
as moral community 11, 20, 65–6,
  67, 72, 74, 76, 122
neighbours of 3, 13, 28–9, 49, 84,
  107, 108
as periphery 2, 47, 65, 66, 84, 96,
  98, 106, 112, 118, 120, 121,
  135
physical aspects of 1, 14, 15, 19,
  21, 23–4, 25, 58
powerlessness, sense of 65–6, 106,
  111, 136
reputation of 12–13, 49, 56, 59,
  65, 67, 107–8
returnees to 2, 124
sense of achievement in 3, 107–8
sense of belonging to 6, 22, 29–30,
  43, 46–8, 73, 83–5, 98,
  104–5, 120
Ireland 7, 22
anthropology of 4, 7, 12, 125,
  128, 132, 136–7
class structure 128
and Irish culture 137
as late modern society 135
political economy of 31, 32, 35,
  84, 110–11
west of 7
Irish State 11, 31, 32, 35, 37, 38, 120,
  130
Irish Urban Cultures 132

Jameson, Fredric 134
jolter 77, 142 n8
Jones, Ruth (shop owner) 92, 94, 116

Jones, Tara 143 n9
junior minister (of education) 114–15,
  118–19

Kimball, S.T. 141 n1
Knauft, B. 143 n4
Knight, John 138 n19
Kilglass 19, 57, 107, 113
Klemperer, Mrs (country resident) 75

Larsen, Sidsel Saugestad 142 n5
Lash, Scott 134
Law, John 140 n7
Loach, Jim (publican) 58
localism, definition of 9
  and locality 9
local knowledge 4, 22, 23, 25, 41,
  56, 58, 69, 83, 84, 104, 122,
  131
  and gossip 72, 81
  as cultural capital 84

mass media 5, 108, 111
McCarthy, Tommy (fisherman) 40
Macdonald, Sharon 139 n20, 139
  n22
McGarrity family (pier) 44, 50
  Barry (fisherman, harbour master)
    50, 60, 61, 64
  Éamon (fisherman) 45, 50
  Lewis (fisherman) 50
  Oliver (fisherman) 50
  Stephen (fisherman) 50
  Ursula (waitress) 69
McGreal family 60
  Eddie (fisherman) 60–4, 67, 73
  Maeve (housewife) 63
MacNamara, Anne 140 n4
Marcus, George 10, 143 n3
mental illness 45, 74
Mewett, Peter 141 n9
Mitchell, J. Clyde 140 n14
modernity 1, 12, 106, 120
  macro-theories of 134–5, 136
Mulligan, Ann (housewife) 91, 92
Murphy, Joan (housewife) 92
Murragh Point 24

Nadel-Klein, Jane 9, 139 n15, 139
  n18, 140 n11

narratives
  construction of 11, 71–4, 84–5,
    95, 127
  content of 38, 72–6, 79, 80–1
  and gossip 72–3, 81, 127
  and morality 72
National school 22, 81, 91, 94, 95,
  113, 114, 115, 118, 126
Neeson family
  Conor (publican) 20, 40, 59, 88
  Máire (publican) 20, 45, 56, 59, 79
nicknames 46

Ochs, Elinor 141 n2
O'Donnell family
  Nuala (publican) 44, 75
  Peadar (publican) 44, 50, 75, 99
  Seamus (publican) 44, 50, 58, 59,
    70, 71, 88
O'Duffy family (farmers) 50
O'Faolain, Nuala 111, 116
O'Hanlon, Michael 138 n7
O'Hara, Patricia 139 n3
O'Toole, Fintan 143 n3, 143 n4

Pálsson, Gísli 10, 139 n21
Parents' Association
  agenda of 92–3, 113
  formation of 91–2
  fund raising by 93, 95
  narrative about 95–6, 97
  organisation of 92–4, 96–7,
    113–16
  and remedial teaching 113–16
  representativeness of 91, 92, 95
  success of 95–6, 104
Parkin, David 142 n7
Peace, Adrian 123, 138 n1, 138 n5,
    139 n14, 140 n5, 140 n9,
    143 n9
Peillon, Michel 143 n7
petite bourgeoisie
  ethos of 106, 120, 136
  as new class 132
  personified 128–32
  and place 131–2
  and private property 8, 17, 52,
    120, 128–9
  status concerns of 7–8, 11, 52, 55,
    130

pier, the
  archetypal family of 43–4, 55
  boats at 24, 46
  camaraderie at 25–6, 36–8, 44,
    63
  conflict in 27–8, 36–8, 44, 53–5,
    57, 59–62, 63, 119
  discourse of 39, 40–1, 42, 53, 62,
    71
  economy of 24–5, 26, 35–8
  identity of 23, 63–4
  location of 23–4
  residences at 25–6, 27–8, 70
  stereotypes about 45, 81
  violence at 26–7, 28
place
  anthropology of 4, 6
  and identity 4, 8, 10, 12, 15, 28,
    29–30, 42–8, 84, 113
  as phantasmagoric 134
  and property 8, 130
  sense of 4, 42–6, 47, 68, 125,
    131–2, 98, 136
  Senses of Place 4
  significance of 1, 4, 7, 8, 12, 23,
    28–30, 131–2
  symbolic properties of 4
playing the *vis-à-vis* 2, 29
political class 109, 114, 115, 118
  alienation from 109, 110, 112,
    120
  and clientalism 110
  and corruption 111
  as gatekeepers 118–9
  as gombeenmen 111, 112
  rhetoric of 110
  and voters 109–10
political economy, relations of 4, 5,
    10, 11, 31–8
Poulantzas, Nicos 7
powerlessness, sense of 65, 106, 109,
    111, 115–16
  and alienation 109
  media influence 111
  reasons for 109–11, 112
  responses to 112–13
priest 22, 23, 76, 77–80, 81, 84, 85,
    88, 90, 91, 96, 101, 116, 117,
    119
public meetings 76, 77–8, 79–80

INDEX

Rabinow, Paul 9, 141 n5
Rapport, Nigel 10, 139 n18
remedial teaching 92, 94, 113, 114,
  115, 118
  bid for 113–15, 118
  failure of 115–16, 119
Richardson, Miles 47
ritual minutiae (of everyday life)
  57–9
Ruane, Rita (shop owner) 20
Ryan, Colm 143 n8

Salazar, Carles 139 n16
sameness, threat of 5–6, 107–8
Scheper-Hughes, Nancy 7, 139 n12
Scherzer, Joel 140 n6
school bus 21, 71, 127
schoolchildren 21, 71
Scully family (business people) 20, 34,
  61, 82, 100
self help 11, 106, 113, 120–1, 130
Senses of Place 4
Silverman, Marilyn 140 n5, 143
  n8
skippers
  and fish buyers 35, 36, 37
  fluid relations of 27
  and sharemen 24–8, 40–1
Smith, M. Estellie 140 n10
sports groups 40, 87–8
St Patrick's Day 51, 99, 107
status concerns 8, 11, 21, 33, 49, 52,
  53, 55
Strathern, Marilyn 139 n18
Sweeney family (village and pier) 51
  Sam 51
Szwed, John F. 141 n5

Taylor, Lawrence 139 n14
Toolin, Adi 85
Tovey, Hilary 143 n2
townland 16, 139 n1

unemployed residents 70, 93
'us' – 'them' opposition 112, 113
U2 101, 103

Varenne, Hervé 143 n6
victualler 19, 20, 23
Village on the Border 142 n2
village, the
  ambience of 19, 21–2, 23, 38
  archetypal family of 44
  businesses in 19–20, 33–5, 40, 69–70
  as common terrain 21
  communal resources of 22–3
  competitiveness in 19–20, 34–6
  discourse of 39, 40, 41, 99
  families in 19–21, 81–2
  location of 19
  reputation of 23
  status concerns in 21
  traffic of 21–2
  wage earners in 21
Vincent, Joan 139 n2
Viney, Michael 139 n13
violence
  physical 26, 28, 45, 57
  symbolic 9, 23, 26
vulnerable residents 74–6, 83

Wadel, Cato 140 n10, 141 n5
wage employment 21, 25, 34, 43, 70,
  129
Westport 21, 34, 39, 57, 58, 60, 61,
  71, 127
Whelan, Mrs Orla (country) 58
White, Leo (farmer) 67
Wilson, Thomas M. 139 n14, 139
  n22, 140 n3, 140 n6
women 50, 89, 117, 126
  on farms 17, 18
  in village 20, 21, 29, 69
  at pier 25, 26, 28, 34, 78, 94, 140 n11
Wright, Eric Olin 7